THE AMERICAN CONSTITUTIONAL SYSTEM

FOUNDATIONS OF AMERICAN GOVERNMENT AND POLITICAL SCIENCE

Joseph P. Harris, Consulting Editor

Revisions and additions have been made to keep this series up to date and to enlarge its scope, but its purpose remains the same as it was on first publication: To provide a group of relatively short treatises dealing with major aspects of government in modern society. Each volume introduces the reader to a major field of political science through a discussion of important issues, problems, processes, and forces and includes at the same time an account of American political institutions. The author of each work is a distinguished scholar who specializes in and teaches the subjects covered. Together the volumes are well adapted to serving the needs of introductory courses in American government and political science.

THE AMERICAN CONSTITUTIONAL SYSTEM

Fourth edition

C. HERMAN PRITCHETT
University of California, Santa Barbara

McGRAW-HILL BOOK COMPANY

New York   St. Louis   San Francisco   Auckland   Düsseldorf   Johannesburg
Kuala Lumpur   London   Mexico   Montreal   New Delhi   Panama
Paris   São Paulo   Singapore   Sydney   Tokyo   Toronto

This book was set in Helvetica by Rocappi, Inc.
The editors were Robert P. Rainier and Phyllis T. Dulan;
the designer was Barbara Ellwood;
the production supervisor was Dennis J. Conroy.
The Murray Printing Company was printer and binder.

Library of Congress Cataloging in Publication Data

Pritchett, Charles Herman, date
    The American constitutional system.

    (Foundations of American government and political science)
    Bibliography: p.
    Includes index.
    1. United States—Constitutional law—Compends.
I. Title. II. Series.
KF4550.Z9P7   1976   342'.73   74-34128
ISBN 0-07-050889-5

THE AMERICAN CONSTITUTIONAL SYSTEM

3 4 5 6 7 8 9 0 MUMU 7 9 8 7

CONTENTS

PREFACE

The fourth edition of this book appears at a time when the American Constitution has been subjected to the gravest test of this century. The Presidency, an office of noble history which has been regarded as one of the great successes of the Constitution, has been exploited by two successive Presidents to the great damage of the country. Lyndon Johnson enmeshed the nation in a land war on the continent of Asia, which was fought with a conscript army, in the tragically mistaken notion that American national interests were involved. The Vietnam war triggered an inflation and other economic problems of unprecedented severity. Richard Nixon took four years to extricate American troops from the Asian quagmire, while at home he was proceeding with the imperial goal of bringing the entire government under his personal control and destroying political opposition by covert and illegal methods.

The ending seemed more suited to a "banana republic" than to the proud American nation—the Vice President exposed as a bribe taker, the President resigning to avoid impeachment for high crimes and misdemeanors. Afterward there were congratulatory comments that "the system had worked." It had been proved that an American President could be forced out of office for abuse of power. The Senate Select Committee on Watergate and the House Judiciary Committee impeachment investigation reflected credit on Congress—a body which has often, and deservedly, been criticized as weak and futile. But the weaknesses of the system have also been highlighted by this experience, and confidence in the ability of government to deal with the crises of our times has been drastically weakened. There is consequently new urgency in a reflective and critical examination of the American constitutional system.

Other studies in this series provide more detail concerning the operation and interrelation of American governmental institutions. This book deals with the document that is the legal basis for all power exercised by the national government of the United States. The purpose of this volume is to describe in broad outlines the structure, functions, powers, and limitations of the American governmental system—the fundamental understandings about American governmental structure and power; to spell out the authoritative foundations for the operative governmental system; and to show how the provisions of the Constitution have been effective in shaping the development of our national institutions.

In all countries the basic framework of public authority is referred to as that country's constitution. The Constitution of the United States is a written document drafted in 1787, which became operative in 1789. It provides for the institutions of the Presidency, the Congress, and the federal courts. It regulates the relationships between the national government and the states and prescribes in more or less general terms their respective spheres of authority. It enumerates legal protections for rights of person and property.

The drafters of the Constitution faced the challenge of planning a new nation with courage and vision. Their wisdom has been proved by time, which has made of the document they framed the oldest written constitution now in effect. However, the credit for this achievement rests not only with the founders, but also with those who have operated the American governmental system and given life to the constitutional provisions over the long period since 1789. This short book cannot undertake to present even a summary of that constitutional history. But it may convey some conception of the Constitution as the instrument and symbol of American democratic government. Never has this aspect of the Constitution been more meaningful nor its proper understanding and appreciation more significant than today.

C. HERMAN PRITCHETT

1 THE AMERICAN CONSTITUTION

The Constitution of the United States of America was drafted between May 14 and September 17, 1787, by 55 men meeting in the city of Philadelphia. It was made effective on June 21, 1788, by the vote of nine state ratifying conventions. Under the governmental system set up by this document, a group of thirteen sparsely populated states strung out along the Atlantic Ocean from Massachusetts to Georgia has developed into one of the great powers of world history. Appropriately, the parchment sheets on which the Constitution was written are preserved as a national shrine in the National Archives at Washington, and the document has come to be regarded with the awe and reverence usually reserved for religious objects.

The Constitution has great value as a symbol of unity for a nation of vast expanse and diverse interests. But as an instrument of government, its language has had to be given life and meaning by the events that have occurred since 1789. Congress animates the Constitution every time it passes a law or holds a hearing. The President construes the Constitution whenever he makes a decision, issues an executive order, or signs a bill into law. The Constitution of the United States is the body of practice built up during the past decades by the executive departments. It is manifested in the historic crises that have been met—Lincoln facing the disintegration of the Union, Franklin D. Roosevelt seeking to restore the national economy, Nixon confronted with the alternatives of impeachment or resignation. It is discoverable equally at lower levels, in the routines and the customs of public life, in what Justice Oliver Wendell Holmes called the inarticulate premises of a nation and a people.

The men who wrote the Constitution were seeking to create a government strong enough for protection against foreign enemies, preservation of the peace internally, and fostering of commercial development and the general welfare. At the same time, they did not want a national government that would be so strong as to obliterate the states or threaten individual rights of liberty and property. They were seeking to establish a system of *constitutional* government.

WHAT IS CONSTITUTIONAL GOVERNMENT?

Until the eighteenth century, the term "constitution" usually meant the general system of laws, institutions, and customs pertaining to the government of a country. The French and American Revolutions, however, brought a new concept of constitution into existence. The constitutional system was no longer to be the product of evolutionary processes. It was not to be deduced from a nation's history or practice. Rather, a constitution was a formal, written instrument, a "social contract" drafted by a representative assembly and ratified by a special procedure for determining public assent. A constitution was the act of a people constituting a government. The constitution brought the government into existence and was its source of authority. The government was the creature of the constitution.

To one accustomed to the older developmental view of constitutions, this was a disturbing departure. The Englishman Arthur Young, writing in 1792, spoke with contempt of the French and American idea of a constitution—"a new term they have adopted; and which they use as if a constitution was a pudding to be made by a recipe." To an Englishman, it was obvious that a constitution could not be made; it had to grow.

Actually, of course, constitutions can combine both qualities. The Constitution of the United States was made in the summer of 1787, but it incorporated a tremendous amount of political experience from the past and has been growing ever since. English history has demonstrated that a democratic political system can develop and individual liberties can be protected as well with a traditional unwritten constitution as with the new-fangled recipe type of constitution. We have even come to see that there may be certain similarities between written and unwritten constitutions—the written one is constantly being reinterpreted and revised by practice and unwritten custom, while the principles of the unwritten constitution are constantly being reduced to writing in statutes, judicial decisions, and constitutional commentaries.

Whether written or unwritten, a constitution has four main purposes. First, it must provide the structure of the governmental system, the organs and institutions of public authority. Second, it must authorize the powers that the government is to possess and allocate them among the various branches and organs. Third, it must state the limitations on governmental power, for the essence of constitutionalism is the maintenance of a balance between authority and liberty, between governmental power and individual rights. Fourth, it must provide for some means other than violent revolution by which the constitutional design can be adapted to future necessities.

THE ARTICLES OF CONFEDERATION

The Constitution drafted in 1787 was actually the second American constitution. The first was the Articles of Confederation, drawn up in 1777 and adopted in 1781. Before that, the colonies had cooperated in their struggle for independence through the Continental Congress, which performed the functions of a de facto government from 1775 to 1781—raising, directing, and financing armies; sending and receiving diplomatic agents; entering into treaties with foreign countries. Whether it had any legal power to perform these actions is another question. The people of the states did not conceive that they had surrendered any of their rights to the Congress, and no state government felt bound by its decisions. Delegates to the Congress, once the states were established, were appointed by the state legislatures and were subject to their instructions.

It was generally agreed that a more effective intercolonial organization was required. A committee was appointed on June 12, 1776, to draw up a plan for a permanent confederation. The Articles of Confederation were adopted and sent to the states in November, 1777. Ratification by every state was required to make them binding, and Maryland, the thirteenth state, did not sign until March 1, 1781, at which time the Articles came into effect.

The framework of government set up by the Articles was quite simple. Virtually all functions were concentrated in a single legislative chamber, called a Congress. There was no second branch of the legislature and no separation of executive from legislative powers. Congress was to appoint such committees and civil officers as might be needed to carry on executive work, and it could provide courts only for the limited purposes of dealing with disputes between states and captures and felonies on the high seas.

The authority of the Congress did not derive from the people, but from the state legislatures that had created it. Each state legislature chose and paid its delegates to the Congress, and each state had one vote. A two-thirds vote of the state delegations was required for the adoption of important measures, and amendments to the Articles required the unanimous consent of the states.

The Articles did specify certain rules of interstate comity to which the states were pledged. But the essential powers necessary to an effective central government were denied to the Confederation. The Congress could not levy taxes; it could only make a "requisition" on each state for its share of the estimated monetary needs of the union. The Congress could not regulate interstate commerce; and although it could make commercial treaties with foreign nations, the states felt free to retaliate against countries that discriminated against their trade. Finally, the Congress could not act directly on the citizens; it had to depend on the state governments for the execution of its measures. The Confederation could scarcely be called a government. As the Articles truthfully stated, it was a league of friendship entered into by sovereign states.

Such a weak government proved quite inadequate to the problems it faced. With no power of taxation, the public finances were soon in a hopeless state. With no power to regulate internal trade, the states taxed each other's goods in discriminatory fashion. Since the Confederation had no powers for dealing with the postwar economic inflation, full pressure of the debtor class fell on the states; and in seven state legislatures, programs authorizing the payment of debts with paper money were adopted. When such a plan was defeated in Massachusetts, farmers under the leadership of Daniel Shays resorted to violence, breaking up court sessions trying debt cases and attempting to seize arms from the government arsenal in Springfield.

Shays' Rebellion was most effective in convincing the conservative and the propertied that there were serious defects in the governments both of the states and the Confederation. The revolutionary enthusiasm for the legislature as the dominant branch of government had diminished. Now responsible citizens were looking for some way of checking the legislatures. The post of state governor was still too weak for this purpose, and a system of judicial review of legislation had not yet been developed. The only effective control over state radicalism appeared to be a strengthening of the central government. In 1785, a meeting of representatives from Virginia and Maryland was held at George Washington's home at Mount Vernon, for the purpose of discussing joint problems of navigation on Chesapeake Bay and the Potomac. Ignoring a provision in the Articles that required congressional consent to all agreements between states, they developed a plan for uniformity of import duties, commercial regulations, and currency in the two states.

When the Maryland legislature accepted these proposals in December, 1785, it suggested that Pennsylvania and Delaware be invited to join in the plan. In Virginia, James Madison saw the possibility of using this initiative to get a general meeting on commercial problems, which the Virginia assembly proposed should meet at Annapolis in September, 1786. Nine states appointed delegates to go to Annapolis, but only five were present at the opening session. They waited three weeks for more delegates and then adjourned. But a report was drafted and sent to every state legislature and to Congress, suggesting that the states designate commissioners to meet in Philadelphia in May, 1787, "to take into consideration the situation of the United States, to devise such further provisions as shall appear to them necessary to render the Constitution of the Federal Government adequate to the exigencies of the Union."

Congress at first ignored the project; but, in February, 1787, it recommended a convention at the time and place already set, to meet for the "sole and express purpose of revising the Articles of Confederation" and of reporting to the Congress such alterations as would "render the federal constitution adequate to the exigencies of government, and the preservation of the union." Thus the official status of the Philadelphia Convention was merely that of a body advisory to Congress.

THE CONSTITUTIONAL CONVENTION

The Constitutional Convention met on May 28, 1787, and continued its deliberations until the completed document was ready for signature on September 17. Some 74 delegates were appointed, but only 55 ever attended the sessions. Every state except Rhode Island was eventually represented. With George Washington as the presiding officer, the delegates were a notable assemblage. They were comparatively young men, only 12 being over fifty-four years of age, and 6 were under thirty-one. Almost half were college graduates. They were men of substance and position in the new country—lawyers, physicians, planters, merchants. Most of them had risked their necks in prominent military or civilian posts during the

Revolution. But the fact that only 8 of the 56 signers of the Declaration of Independence were in the Constitutional Convention is evidence that making a constitution enlisted different talents and interests from those required for making a revolution.

In the Convention, votes were cast by states. The proceedings were secret, and knowledge of what occurred is very largely due to the extensive notes that James Madison kept. Soon after the delegates assembled, a complete and far-reaching plan for establishing a new national government was presented by the Virginia delegation. The Virginia Plan called for a bicameral legislature, with representation in both houses on the basis of population. The congress was to have sweeping legislative powers of its own as well as the power to veto all state laws that it regarded as going beyond state authority. The congress was to select the national executive, and a national judiciary was also contemplated. The executive and judiciary combined could constitute a "council of revision" with power to veto acts of the congress.

Delegates who found these proposals too sweeping countered with the so-called New Jersey Plan, which was more on the pattern of the Articles of Confederation. There would continue to be a unicameral legislature in which each state would have equal representation, but the authority of the central government would be substantially increased by the addition of power to tax and to regulate commerce. Another important advance in this plan was that federal laws and treaties were to be binding on the states. A federal executive and judiciary were also provided.

The Convention after assembling turned itself into a committee of the whole and for three weeks mulled over these two plans. The New Jersey proposal was defeated on June 19. The members then reverted from committee status and, as a convention, began to go over again the various features of the Virginia Plan. One month of discussion produced agreement on a substantial number of points, so that on July 23 the Convention voted to set up a committee of detail which would draft a constitution embodying the principles agreed upon. This group, however, did more than redraft the Convention's resolutions into documentary form. It expanded some of the resolutions and developed some entirely new provisions. The resulting document was presented to the Convention on August 6 and was the subject of further extended discussion. On September 17, the Constitution was signed by 39 of the 42 delegates present.

AMERICAN POLITICAL IDEAS

The ideas that went into the Constitution of the United States were drawn from the whole European political heritage of the new nation. The ideas themselves were not especially new nor were they creative inventions of the assembly. The genius of the Convention was in its practicality and willingness to compromise dogmatic principles rather than in any theoretical brilliance.

The Declaration of Independence has been generally regarded as the cornerstone of the American system of ideas about government, and the preeminent statement of American political theory. The basic conceptions had come from the English philosopher John Locke, but the doctrines were sharpened and intensified by the experience of resistance to British rule. These principles were so much a part of American thinking that the Declaration referred to them as "self-evident." In addition to the Declaration, the constitutions of the new American states that were adopted between 1776 and 1780 abound in statements of the current political theory.

The first principle of the political thought of the time was that men are by nature endowed with certain inalienable rights. This conception assumed that a state of nature exists before the establishment of civil government. In this primeval condition all men are free, in the sense that they are subject to no one and are equal in the right to rule themselves. A body of natural rights belongs to them as men, including the right to "life, liberty, and the pursuit of happiness." These rights not only antedate the existence of government; they are superior to it in authority.

The exercise of coercive power by governments over men born free and equal can be justified only by the consent of the governed. The process as expressed by the Massachusetts Bill of Rights was that "the body politic is formed by a voluntary association of individuals: it is a social compact by which the whole people covenants with each citizen, and each citizen with the whole people, that all shall be governed by certain laws for the common good." The exact nature of the contract on which government was based and the circumstances under which it was entered into were little discussed; but this concept was given a sense of reality by the numerous written compacts which had figured in American development, especially the Mayflower Compact of 1620 and the colonial charters. The slogan "no taxation without representation" was a particular application of the consent theory, with roots deep in English constitutional history.

Government is created by contract to serve the welfare of the people. To quote again the Massachusetts document, the aim of government is "to secure the existence of the body politic, to protect it, and to furnish the individuals who compose it with the power of enjoying in safety and tranquillity their natural rights, and the blessings of life." A government that fails to serve the ends for which it was set up has breached the contract under which it was established and forfeited the loyalty of its citizens. Thus the right of revolution, obviously fundamental to legitimizing the American action, was established. The Declaration of Independence stated the case as follows: "Whenever any form of government becomes destructive of these ends, it is the right of the people to alter or to abolish it, and to institute new government, laying its foundation on such principles and organizing its powers in such forms, as to them shall seem most likely to effect their safety and happiness."

The consequences of these basic political ideas quickly became visible in the constitutions adopted by the new states after 1776. Governmental power was limited in several ways. The royal governors had been the symbol of tyranny; and so the executive office in the new constitutions was deliberately weakened, while the legislature, symbol of resistance to foreign rule, was strengthened. In eight states the governor was chosen by the legislature, he had only a one-year term in ten states, his appointing power was generally limited, and he had the veto power in only three states. The one-year rule was common for all officials, not only for governors; as John Adams said, "where annual elections end, there tyranny begins."

The democratic theory professed in the new constitutions was not consistently practiced, however. Under the colonial government, the lower classes had been rather generally excluded from political life. The revolutionary movement for a time gave promise of bringing the back-country folk and the unfranchised workers into the stream of politics, but actually the circle of power holders was little changed in the new state governments. Property and religious qualifications for office holding were general. Indeed, property, religious, and racial limitations were seemingly not regarded as inconsistent with the rights of man or the principles of political philosophy so eloquently stated in the Declaration of Independence.

CONSTITUTIONAL PRINCIPLES

These ideas were the foundation for the constitutional principles embodied in the instrument signed on September 17, 1787. First of all, the Constitution established a *republican* form of government. The monarchial principle had of course been completely discredited by colonial experience with George III, and republicanism was the revolutionary doctrine of the era. But there was considerable question in the minds of the founders as to how far the republican or representative principle should be carried. Direct election was provided for the House of Representatives, but the Senate was to be chosen by the state legislatures. Likewise, only a few of the delegates favored direct election of the President. Election by Congress was strongly supported, but eventually the Convention agreed on selection by electors chosen in each state as the legislature of that state might direct.

The only place where the term "republican" appears in the Constitution is in Article IV, which provides that the United States shall guarantee "a republican form of government" to every state in the Union, but the term is not there defined. Some have argued that since the United States was created as a republic, it is a serious mistake to think of our government as a "democracy." This position is usually taken by conservatives who treasure the aristocratic manifestations in the initial constitutional provisions and who disapprove of modern trends toward egalitarianism, direct democracy, and mass society in general. Unquestionably, an evolution has gone on which may be described as a change from a republic to a representative democracy, but this development has occurred within the framework of constitutional principles.

Second, the Constitution set up a *federal* system. The delegates were in general agreement that a stronger central government had to be formed. Although their instructions were simply to revise the Articles of Confederation, it was obvious that the goals they had in mind required more fundamental changes.

Under the Articles, the central establishment was a confederation, a mere league of states, each of which retained its sovereign powers. The Constitution set up a new central government, which got its authority directly from the people, and was to exercise its powers directly on the people. The states retained their status and such of their powers as were not transferred to the national government. Naturally a central consideration at the Convention was to decide what powers would be so transferred and how the division of functions would be described and enforced. The operation of a two-level governmental system has presented endless constitutional issues, the more important of which are discussed in Chapter 2; and one aspect of the relationship between the central government and the states had to be settled by a bloody civil war.

The federal principle was also at issue in the organization of the Congress. The large states, such as Virginia, Massachusetts, and Pennsylvania, were confident of their position in the new government and so supported the centralizing provisions of the Virginia Plan. The small states feared the dominance of their larger neighbors and wanted protection for their interests.

It was generally accepted that the House of Representatives would be elected by the people and that membership would be proportionate to population. The Senate was to be elected by the state legislatures, and the large states wanted representation by population here also. But in the Congress under the Confederation and in the Convention itself, each state had one vote, and the small states would not agree to a plan that did not preserve their status in some way. Finally on July 16 the Convention adopted the principle of equal state representation in the Senate by a vote of 5 to 4.

Third, the Constitution adopted the *separation-of-powers* principle. The first sentence of Article I vested "all legislative powers" in Congress, and the first sentences of Articles II and III similarly vested executive and judicial power in the President and in the courts, respectively. Each branch had its particular task—making the law, administering the law, enforcing the law. The division was in accord with the goal of limited government and was intended to make abuse of official power less likely.

For additional insurance and with an eye to the realities of governmental operation, the founders infringed on strict separation-of-powers theory by a system of checks and balances that enabled each branch to have some say in the operation of the other two. The President could veto laws and appoint federal justices. The Senate could confirm executive and judicial appointments and ratify treaties. Congress could control the kinds of cases to be heard by the Supreme Court. The courts could interpret congressional statutes and pass on the validity of executive acts.

Finally, basic to all the other ideas was that of *constitutionalism* itself, the conception that government power must be both authorized and limited by undertakings arrived at in advance, consented to by those affected, and given continuing validity by appropriate enforcement processes. The rule of law and of representative institutions with defined authority was to stand as a guarantee of individual liberty against the exercise of arbitrary governmental power.

RATIFICATION

The drafters of the Constitution realized that ratification of the document would present grave difficulties. The Articles of Confederation provided that revisions could be made only by a favorable vote of Congress and the approval of the legislatures in all thirteen states. Rhode Island had not even sent delegates to the Convention, and there were other states where approval of the new Constitution was doubtful. Public opinion at the time was badly divided on the need for a stronger central government. In general, the rural areas, the farmers and backwoodsmen, were quite suspicious, as a Massachusetts farmer put it, of "these lawyers, and men of learning, and moneyed men, that talk so finely, and gloss over matters so smoothly, to make us poor illiterate people swallow down the pill."

The drafters faced this problem boldly and developed in Article VII an entirely extralegal solution. They provided first that the Constitution should become effective on ratification by nine states. Second, ratification was to be by conventions in the states elected for this specific purpose. Third, the Constitution was not to be presented to the Congress before being submitted to the states.

The use of state conventions for ratification purposes could be justified as providing a more democratic foundation for the new government, but it was also a practical means of bypassing hostile state legislatures unlikely to give up their own powers. The pro-Constitution forces sought to get the conventions elected as promptly as possible, before the opposition had a chance to organize. About three-fourths of the male white citizens over twenty-one failed to vote in the elections for convention delegates, Charles A. Beard estimates, either on account of their indifference or their disfranchisement by property qualifications.

One of the legacies of the ratification campaign was the most famous commentary on American government, *The Federalist.* These essays were newspaper articles written to influence the vote in the doubtful state of New York by James Madison, Alexander Hamilton, and John Jay. Their discussions of the proposed Constitution have been generally thought to have had great influence at the time and have been widely accepted as authoritative guides to constitutional interpretation.

The Constitution was ratified by a wide majority in seven of the state conventions, but in the important states of Massachusetts, Virginia, and New York the voting was close. North Carolina and Rhode Island were the last two states to ratify. If a unanimous vote had been required to make the Constitution effective, it is probable that they would have stayed out, thus frustrating the entire effort.

The absence of a bill of rights was the most widespread criticism in the ratifying conventions, and in several doubtful states the promise that a bill of rights would be added was instrumental in securing the votes needed for ratification.

AMENDING THE CONSTITUTION

Since the Constitution was ratified, tremendous changes have occurred in the United States and the world. Technical discoveries and inventions have affected the life of the country. Population has multiplied manyfold. The political party has undergone a transformation from a despised source of faction to an indispensable instrument of representative government. Public agencies have taken over responsibilities undreamed of in the eighteenth century. Standards of public morality have changed. How is a government of continental proportions and worldwide responsibilities, with a budget of more than $350 billion, to be accommodated within the confines of a document drafted almost two centuries earlier for the sparse population of thirteen isolated states along the Atlantic seaboard?

One answer is the framers of the Constitution were wise enough, and good enough politicians, to avoid the evil of too great specificity in drafting key provisions of the document. Their general intent was to stick to the fundamentals and leave the implementation to subsequent legislative decision. In places, they remained deliberately vague and so avoided crystallization of opposition forces that would have been able to mobilize against concrete proposals. Thus no departmental setup for the executive branch was written into the Constitution. The question of a system of lower courts was left to Congress, as were the matters of presidential succession beyond the Vice President, and the time, place, and manner of electing representatives and senators. The powers given to the President and to Congress were typically stated in broad language.

Nevertheless, no amount of drafting skill could be expected to eliminate the necessity of revision and development to adapt the Constitution to the unforeseen and the unforeseeable. This adaptation has taken two forms—constitutional amendment and constitutional interpretation.

The presence of the amending clause was one of the factors that led Thomas Jefferson, originally inclined to oppose the Constitution, to decide in its favor. Since 1789, the procedures of Article V have been utilized to add 26 amendments to the Constitution. The first 10 of these amendments were drafted to meet the widespread protests against the absence of a bill of rights in the original Constitution and were adopted in 1791.

Only 14 amendments have been added in the century since the Civil War. The Thirteenth, Fourteenth, and Fifteenth Amendments were adopted shortly after that conflict to abolish slavery and to protect the rights of the newly freed Negroes. The Sixteenth and Seventeenth Amendments, both adopted in 1913, reflected the progressive political philosophy of the early twentieth century by authorizing the federal income tax and providing for direct popular election of senators. The Eighteenth Amendment (1919), authorizing national prohibition, was repealed by the Twenty-first (1933). The Twenty-second Amendment (1951) limited the President to two terms in office, and the Twenty-third (1961) gave residents of the District of Columbia the right to vote in presidential elections. The Twenty-fourth Amendment (1964) abolished the use of the poll tax as a prerequisite for voting in elections for federal offices, the Twenty-fifth (1967) adopted improved arrangements for presidential inability and succession, and the Twenty-sixth (1971) gave the vote to eighteen-year-olds.

Of the two methods that Article V provides for proposing amendments—by a two-thirds majority of each house of Congress or by a convention summoned by Congress at the request of the legislatures of two-thirds of the states—only the former has been employed. Since a constitutional convention has never been called under Article V, there is no agreement as to the many questions that would arise concerning operation of such a convention.

If petitions were actually received from two-thirds of the state legislatures, there would be no means of forcing Congress to call the requested amending convention, and it can be anticipated that Congress would not welcome such an infringement on what has become one of its own prerogatives. If Congress did acquiesce, it would have to provide by statute for calling the convention. Whether legislation could in any way limit the powers of the convention is questionable, however. After assembling, the delegates might undertake to consider amendments to any part of the Constitution or even propose an entirely new document, as the Convention of 1787 did.

In view of all the uncertainties surrounding the convention provision, it seems unlikely that the Constitution will ever be amended by this method. After the Supreme Court ruled in 1964 that members of both houses in state legislatures must be elected from districts equal in population, Sen. Everett Dirksen led an effort to secure a constitutional amendment that would modify this holding. Failing twice to secure the necessary two-thirds vote in the Senate, he helped organize a national campaign to persuade three-fourths of the state legislatures to request Congress to call a convention for this purpose. In fact, 33 of the necessary 34 legislatures did respond favorably, and this near miss served an important educational function in making evident the perils in the convention device.

The ratification of all the amendments to the Constitution except one has been by vote of three-fourths of the state legislatures. Only in the case of the Twenty-first Amendment, which repealed the Eighteenth, did Congress require the use of state conventions. The reason for this exception was the fear in Congress that the overrepresentation in the state legislatures of rural areas, which tended to be "dry," might imperil adoption of the amendment, whereas conventions would more equitably represent the views of the urban areas.

Perhaps the most striking fact about the amending process is the infrequency with which it has been used. Excluding the initial ten amendments, which must be considered practically part of the original Constitution, amendments have been adopted at a rate of less than one per decade. Following the Civil War amendments, there was a period of more than 40 years during which the Constitution appeared unamendable. This was an era of agrarian discontent, industrial unrest, and growing interest in political and economic reforms. The conservatism of the Supreme

Court, symbolized by its invalidation of the income tax in 1895, made constitutional amendment seem a necessary step toward achieving liberal legislative goals.

In 1913, however, the long liberal campaign for the income tax and direct election of senators succeeded, and the women's suffrage amendment followed shortly thereafter. Also, adoption of the Eighteenth Amendment revealed the possibility of a small but dedicated pressure group exploiting the amending machinery successfully. With six amendments added to the Constitution between 1913 and 1933, the amending process no longer seemed so formidable. Moreover, the liberalization of the Supreme Court's views by President Franklin D. Roosevelt's appointments substantially eliminated liberal interest in further amendments.

After the 1930s, pressure for amendments to the Constitution came principally from conservative political quarters. The increase in executive power and congressional expenditures, the acceptance of new welfare functions domestically and new responsibilities internationally by the federal government, the reduced role of the states, and liberal tendencies on the Supreme Court were all factors stimulating conservative recourse to the amending process. During the 1950s, the Bricker amendment to limit the federal government's power to enter into international agreements, as well as a proposal to place a ceiling on federal income taxation, were conservative measures that failed of adoption. In the 1960s, efforts to override the Supreme Court's decisions on "one man, one vote" and Bible reading in the public schools were defeated. The only amendment actually secured by this drive was the Twenty-second, limiting the President to two terms.

The more recent amendments have returned to the old liberal pattern. Three of the four adopted since 1961 provide for extension of the franchise, while the potential Twenty-seventh Amendment guaranteeing equal rights for women was still in 1975 before the state legislatures for ratification.

INTERPRETING THE CONSTITUTION

A second method for adapting the Constitution to changing conditions is the device of constitutional interpretation. In fact, the possibility of gradual modification of constitutional meanings to meet new times and new necessities is the principal reason why resort to formal amendment has been relatively infrequent.

The process of constitutional adaptation is one that goes on at many levels and in many contexts. There are adaptations that develop on an entirely unplanned basis in the form of usage or customs or methods of procedure or institutions. Perhaps the most striking example in American history is the prompt development after 1789 of a party system, for which the framers had not planned and which in fact they had taken some pains to try to prevent. The party system, with its tickets for President and Vice President, immediately required the remedial provisions of the Twelfth

Amendment, but in no other respect has the written Constitution been changed to recognize the realities of party government. The development of committees in Congress, the rise of the Cabinet, the use of executive agreements instead of treaties, the assumption that representatives must be residents of the districts they represent in Congress—these and many other customs and usages were evolutionary adjustments of the constitutional system to practical problems with which it was confronted.

A much more intentional and sophisticated type of constitutional interpretation goes on in the decision making of the executive and legislative branches. When President Kennedy recommended federal financial aid to the schools in 1961, he announced his view that public aid to religious schools was unconstitutional, and the Secretary of Health, Education, and Welfare presented to Congress a legal brief indicating the administration's view as to what the constitutional problems were in federal aid to education.

This legislation failed of adoption, largely because no financial aid was provided for religious schools. But President Johnson, following a different constitutional theory, linked aid to education with the war on poverty and secured adoption of the Elementary and Secondary Education Act of 1965, which provided financial assistance by way of the public schools to all children in poverty-impacted areas, thus enabling students in religious schools to benefit by the program without directly raising the religious issue.

The most highly rationalized type of constitutional interpretation is that engaged in by judges, and particularly by the Supreme Court of the United States. Circumstances have given the Supreme Court recognition as the "official" interpreter of the Constitution, and its rulings are accepted as the best evidence of constitutional meanings. Although the Supreme Court and its members have often been attacked for individual decisions, judicial interpretation of the Constitution has been generally regarded as an essential safeguard of the constitutional system.

SUMMARY

The Constitution of the United States was drafted to provide a national government that would be strong enough to protect and develop those interests of defense, commercial welfare, and domestic security which the states were separately unable to achieve. The men who made it were generally of the opinion that government is a "necessary evil"; they were jealous of their individual rights and they had strong loyalties to their states. But experience had convinced them that if they did not all hang together they would all hang separately, and so the case for a central "government of powers" was clear to the leaders of opinion.

With all the conflicting interests that were involved, however, the Constitution had to be a product of compromises. Whereas individual liberties were of great concern to the drafters, their language was not explicit enough to satisfy the country; and a detailed bill of rights had to be added as a necessary condition to ratification. The fact that the framers created a government strong enough for national protection and advancement, at the same time preserving a significant role for the states and safeguarding the rights of individuals, is eloquent testimony to their success.

REVIEW QUESTIONS

1 What novel problems did written constitutions create?

2 What are the main functions of a constitution?

3 What were the essential features of governmental organization under the Articles of Confederation?

4 Why was the Constitutional Convention called?

5 Contrast the two principal plans presented to the convention.

6 What were the basic political ideas of the Constitution?

7 Why was the Constitution not submitted to the state legislatures for ratification?

8 Why has the Constitution been amended so seldom?

9 Suggest some of the problems that might be faced if Congress ever summoned a convention to propose amendments to the Constitution.

10 How has the Constitution been kept up to date?

2 THE FEDERAL SYSTEM

In essence, American federalism is a form of political organization in which the exercise of power is divided between two levels of government, each having the use of those powers as a matter of right, and each acting on the same citizen body. The delegates to the Constitutional Convention were aware of the historical applications of a federal form of government in ancient Greece and modern Switzerland, but the federal system for which they provided was not the result of a preexisting political theory being written into law. It was, rather, the product of colonial practices under which local governments had been allowed considerable autonomy, and the political compromises at the convention between those delegates who wished to draft a charter for a strong central government and those who simply desired to improve the existing Articles of Confederation.

THE FEDERAL POWER POSITION

A strong central government could be created only by taking powers away from the existing state governments and delegating them to the central government. Thus the United States is often referred to as a government of "delegated powers." The most significant listing of powers delegated to Congress is found in Article I, section 8, ranging all the way from the punishment of counterfeiting to the declaration of war. These specifically stated authorizations covered all the subjects that occurred to the founders as necessary for the new central government to possess. Moreover, the authorizations were typically stated very broadly, as, for example, the power to regulate commerce and to levy taxes.

Backing up these broad grants of specific powers, moreover, was the general authorization to Congress in the last clause of Article I, section 8, "to make all laws which shall be necessary and proper for carrying into execution the foregoing powers." The relationship of clause 18 to the enumerated powers preceding it quickly became the subject of controversy between Federalists and Jeffersonians, between broad and strict constructionists. The issue was joined over Hamilton's plan for a national bank, as presented to the First Congress. There was no authorization in the Constitution for Congress to create a bank; in fact, the convention had specifically refused to grant to Congress even a restricted power to create corporations. On President Washington's invitation, Hamilton and Jefferson submitted their respective views on whether he should sign the bill, and their statements still stand as classic expositions of divergent theories of constitutional interpretation.

Jefferson emphasized the "necessary" in the necessary and proper clause. Since all the enumerated powers could be carried out without a bank, it was not necessary and consequently not authorized. Hamilton, on the other hand, argued that the powers granted to Congress included the right to employ "all the *means* requisite and fairly applicable to the attainment of the *ends* of such power," unless they were specifically forbidden or immoral or contrary to the "essential ends of political society." The Hamilton theory of a broad and liberal interpretation of congressional power was successful in persuading Washington to sign the bank bill, and it has generally predominated in subsequent constitutional development.

In 1819, Chief Justice John Marshall gave the definitive statement of this view in the great case of *McCulloch v. Maryland,* in which congressional authority to create a bank—the Bank of the United States, incorporated by statute in 1816—was again the issue. Marshall found implied congressional power to establish a bank in the expressly granted powers to collect taxes, to borrow money, to regulate commerce, to declare and conduct a war; for "it may with great reason be contended, that a government, entrusted with such ample powers, on the due execution of which the happiness and prosperity of the nation so vitally depends, must also be entrusted with ample means for their execution." A corporation was such a means. "It is never the end for which other powers are exercised."

Marshall analyzed the necessary and proper clause at length. He rejected the strict Jeffersonian interpretation, which "would abridge, and almost annihilate this useful and necessary right of the legislature to select the means." His final, and famous, conclusion was: "Let the end be legitimate, let it be within the scope of the constitution, and all means which are appropriate, which are plainly adapted to that end, which are not prohibited, but consistent with the letter and spirit of the constitution, are constitutional."

In considering the power position of Congress, it should also be noted that the Constitution made a few specific prohibitions on exercise of federal power, such as suspending the writ of habeas corpus or levying direct taxes without enumeration. When the Bill of Rights was adopted in 1791, the extensive prohibitions of the first eight amendments were added to this group of restrictions on federal power.

THE STATE POWER POSITION

In the Constitution as originally drafted, no effort was made to state any general formula reserving to the states the powers not delegated to Congress. That nondelegated powers remained with the states was regarded as so obvious that it did not need to be spelled out. However, specific assurances were demanded during the ratification debates, which were met by adding the Tenth Amendment: "The powers not delegated to the

United States by the Constitution, nor prohibited by it to the States, are reserved to the States respectively, or to the people."

The Tenth Amendment was clearly not intended to be a limitation on federal powers, for it excepts from its effect "powers . . . delegated to the United States." Nevertheless, advocates of states' rights and antagonists of federal authority have periodically attempted to create out of the Tenth Amendment barriers to federal action authorized elsewhere in the Constitution. On the Supreme Court under Chief Justice Roger B. Taney, the doctrine of "dual federalism" asserted that the two levels of government were coequal sovereignties and that authority delegated to the national government was limited by the powers reserved to the states in the Tenth Amendment.

The theory of dual federalism can be best illustrated by the Supreme Court's decision in *Hammer v. Dagenhart* (1918). Congress had passed in 1916 a statute forbidding the transportation in interstate commerce of goods produced by the labor of children below certain ages. This was clearly a regulation of commerce, and the Supreme Court had approved earlier statutes making use of this same power for other purposes. But in the *Hammer* case the Court majority asserted that the age at which children could go to work in factories was a local matter that had been reserved to the states under the Tenth Amendment. For the five-judge majority, Justice William R. Day wrote: "The grant of authority over a purely federal matter was not intended to destroy the local power always existing and carefully reserved to the States in the Tenth Amendment." He went on to say that in interpreting the Constitution it should never be forgotten that "the powers not expressly delegated to the National Government are reserved" to the states and the people by the Tenth Amendment.

To arrive at this conclusion, Justice Day had to misquote the amendment; the term "expressly" does not appear in its text. Indeed, when the Tenth Amendment was under consideration in the First Congress the anti-Federalists had tried to insert the word "expressly," but had been voted down. In any case, the commerce power had been expressly delegated to Congress. These errors did not go unchallenged. Speaking for the four dissenters, Justice Oliver Wendell Holmes declared: "I should have thought that the most conspicuous decisions of this Court had made it clear that the power to regulate commerce and other constitutional powers could not be cut down or qualified by the fact that it might interfere with the carrying out of the domestic policy of any State." Eventually, in 1941, the Supreme Court overruled the faulty majority opinion and established Holmes's position as the law of the Constitution.

THE SUPREME LAW OF THE LAND

The Constitution thus set up ground rules for the federal system by an allocation of authority to the two levels of government. But this was not enough. Conflicts over the division of functions were bound to occur between the states and the nation. To make the federal system work, there needed to be rules for deciding such contests and an umpire to apply those rules. The principal rule of this kind supplied by the Constitution is the "supremacy clause" of Article VI: "This Constitution, and the laws of the United States which shall be made in pursuance thereof; and all treaties made, or which shall be made, under the authority of the United States, shall be the supreme law of the land; and the judges in every state shall be bound thereby, anything in the Constitution or laws of any state to the contrary notwithstanding."

The effectiveness of this section was early demonstrated in the case of *McCulloch v. Maryland* already mentioned. The specific issue was the validity of a tax levied by the Maryland legislature on the federally chartered Bank of the United States. The cashier of the Baltimore branch of the Bank refused to pay the tax and was convicted of violating the law by the state courts. The Supreme Court unanimously upheld the Bank's position, Chief Justice Marshall basing his opinion squarely on the supremacy clause. "If any one proposition could command the universal assent of mankind," he wrote, "we might expect it would be this: that the government of the Union, though limited in its powers, is supreme within its sphere of action." Consequently, no state had any power "to retard, impede, burden, or in any manner control, the operations of the constitutional laws enacted by congress."

When Congress enters a field in which it is authorized to act, then, its legislation voids all incompatible state regulations. In practical terms, however, the question whether Congress has preempted a given area is a difficult one, since federal statutes seldom state whether all local rules on the matter are suspended. It falls ultimately to the Supreme Court to determine the relation of federal and state statutes.

In *Pennsylvania v. Nelson* (1956), Chief Justice Earl Warren attempted to codify the tests which the Court has used to guide such decisions. First, is the scheme of federal regulation so. pervasive as to make it a reasonable inference that Congress has left no room for the states? Second, do the federal statutes touch a field in which the interest of the national government is so dominant that it must be assumed to preclude state action on the same subject? Third, does enforcement of the state act present a serious danger of conflict with the administration of the federal program?

In the *Nelson* case, a conviction for violation of the Pennsylvania sedition act had been reversed by the state supreme court on the ground that a federal sedition act (the Smith Act of 1940) had occupied the field and superseded the state law. The United States Supreme Court agreed. Using the three criteria just suggested, Warren concluded that Congress had taken over the entire task of protecting the federal government from seditious conduct when it passed the Smith Act, even though no express intention to exclude the states was stated in that statute.

THE UMPIRE

The umpire for deciding conflicts between state and nation over the constitutional division of functions is, as we have just seen, the Supreme

Court. That the enforcement of the principle of federal supremacy was essentially a judicial task was implied in the supremacy clause. The First Congress saw the necessity to spell out the Supreme Court's powers of review over the decisions of state courts so that the supremacy of the federal constitution could be preserved. The Judiciary Act of 1789, in section 25, provided for such review of final judgments or decrees in state courts in three classes of cases: (1) where the validity of a federal law or treaty was "drawn in question," and the decision was *against* its validity; (2) where a state statute was questioned as "repugnant to the constitution, treaties or laws of the United States," and the decision was *in favor* of its validity; and (3) where the construction of the federal Constitution, treaty, or statute was drawn in question, and the decision was *against* the title, right, privilege, or exemption claimed.

These categories were all based on the principle that if the Constitution and laws of the United States were to be observed, the Supreme Court would have to have an opportunity to review decisions of state courts that ruled adversely on asserted federal rights. Courts in some states, particularly Virginia, did not submit without a struggle to the idea that their decisions were subject to review by the Supreme Court. However, the Supreme Court's authority was firmly asserted and established by two great early decisions, *Martin v. Hunter's Lessee* (1816) and *Cohens v. Virginia* (1821).

STATE RESISTANCE TO FEDERAL AUTHORITY

The nature of the federal union created by the Constitution was a perennial matter of controversy that finally brought on a tragic civil war. The issue in 1861 was slavery, but earlier there had been several other controversies that had led to the elaboration of theories of state resistance to federal authority.

One resulted from passage by a Federalist Congress of the Alien and Sedition Acts of 1798. These statutes were aimed at the opposition Jeffersonian party and at the partisans of France, many of whom were aliens. The laws imposed harsh restrictions on aliens and punished criticism of the government. Jefferson and Madison, searching for a basis to attack these laws, drafted the so-called Virginia and Kentucky Resolutions and secured their adoption by the legislatures of these two states.

The doctrine of these resolutions sounded rather radical. In the Kentucky Resolutions, Jefferson seemed to argue that the states had an "equal right" with the federal government to interpret the Constitution, and that they could nullify acts passed by Congress which they deemed unauthorized. Madison in the Virginia Resolutions suggested that the states could "interpose" their authority to prevent the exercise by the federal government of powers not granted by the Constitution.

This language about nullification and interposition sounds more threatening than Jefferson and Madison probably intended. Certainly, they were deadly serious in their beliefs that the Federalist Congress had passed legislation prohibited by the Constitution and in wanting to organize resistance to it. But both sets of resolutions were vague as to how such resistance was to be carried out. They hardly meant to assert that the Union was a system of fully sovereign states, a confederation from which each state could retire at any time. Jefferson's victory over the Federalists in the election of 1800, due in no small part to popular resentment over the Alien and Sedition Acts, terminated this cause of conflict.

A much more clearly elaborated theory of nullification and resistance to national authority was stated in 1828 by John C. Calhoun as a rationalization of Southern opposition to the continual increase in tariff rates between 1816 and 1828. Calhoun was alarmed at the open talk of secession in the South, and offered the doctrine of nullification as a substitute, contending that his plan was a logical extension of the Virginia and Kentucky Resolutions.

Calhoun held that the Constitution was a compact formed by "sovereign and independent communities." The national government was not a party to the compact but an emanation from it, "a joint commission, appointed to superintend and administer the interests in which all are jointly concerned, but having, beyond its proper sphere, no more power than if it did not exist." He thought, however, that mere recognition of the right of interposition would probably "supersede the necessity of its exercise, by impressing on the movements of the Government that moderation and justice so essential to harmony and peace, in a country of such vast extent and diversity of interests as ours."

In 1832, South Carolina carried this theory to the point of action by passing a statute purporting to nullify the federal tariff acts of 1828 and 1832. President Andrew Jackson immediately challenged this action, saying that the power of nullification was "incompatible with the existence of the Union, contradicted expressly by the letter of the Constitution, unauthorized by its spirit, inconsistent with every principle on which it was founded, and destructive of the great object for which it was formed." He sent federal vessels into Charleston Harbor to enforce the tariff, but passage of a compromise tariff bill with lower rates made it possible for South Carolina to withdraw its nullification statute.

The final test remained. In the years preceding the Civil War, with the controversies over slavery and the tariff going on around them, Southern statesmen shifted their ground from the right of nullification to secession as a means to preserve their economic life and social institutions. For Calhoun, secession was justified as a final remedy to preserve states' rights. According to his theory, after a state had interposed its authority to prevent federal action, the federal government could appeal to the amending process. If three-fourths of the states upheld the federal claim, the matter was settled as far as those states were concerned. But the dissenting state was not obliged to acquiesce in all instances:

That a State, as a party to the constitutional compact, has the right to secede,—acting in the same capacity in which it ratified the constitution,—cannot, with any show of reason, be denied by any one who regards the constitution as a compact,—if a power should be inserted by the amending power, which would radically change the character of the constitution, or the nature of the system.

Lincoln's decision to use force to keep the Southern states in the Union and the victory of the North in the Civil War closed the debate over the legality of secession. After the war, the Supreme Court tidied up a bit in *Texas v. White* (1869). The case hinged on the question whether or not Texas had ever left the Union, and the Court held:

> When, therefore, Texas became one of the United States, she entered into an indissoluble relation. . . . The act which consummated her admission into the Union was something more than a compact; it was the incorporation of a new member into the political body. And it was final. The union between Texas and the other States was as complete, as perpetual, and as indissoluble as the union between the original States.

Chief Justice Salmon P. Chase summed up the principle involved: "The Constitution, in all its provisions, looks to an indestructible Union, composed of indestructible States."

In 1956, the dust was blown off the doctrines of interposition and nullification, as they were invoked by several Southern states in protest against the Supreme Court's decision invalidating racial segregation in the schools. In its act of nullification the state of Alabama laid down the basic premise of its action:

> *Whereas* the states, being the parties to the constitutional compact, it follows of necessity that there can be no tribunal above their authority to decide, in the last resort, whether the compact made by them be violated; and, consequently, they must decide themselves, in the last resort, such questions as may be of sufficient magnitude to require their interposition.

Such principles are of course in flat contradiction to the history and nature of the federal system and, while periodically invoked by angry state officials, have been uniformly rejected.

FEDERAL OBLIGATIONS TO THE STATES

Of the various obligations that the Constitution imposes on the federal government with respect to the states, only one has actually involved significant federal action. This is the responsibility of the United States to prevent domestic violence.

On application of a state legislature or of the state executive, if the legislature cannot be convened, the United States must guarantee a state against "domestic violence" under Article IV, section 4. On at least sixteen occasions the states have sought federal assistance in suppressing domestic violence, a notable instance being the dispatch of troops by President Lyndon B. Johnson to quell the Detroit riots of 1967 at the request of Gov. George Romney.

A request from the state is not necessary, however, when domestic violence threatens the enforcement of national laws. Article I, section 8 authorizes Congress to provide for calling forth the militia to execute the laws of the Union, suppress insurrection, or repel invasion. Under this authority, President Grover Cleveland sent troops into Chicago in 1894 during the Pullman strike to keep the trains running. Likewise, President Dwight D. Eisenhower in 1957 sent federal troops to control violence in Little Rock and enforce federal court orders for desegregation of the local high school, and in 1962 President John F. Kennedy used federal marshals and the national guard to put down violence on the University of Mississippi campus caused by a court order admitting a black student to the university.

Other obligations of the federal government toward the states are to maintain equal representation of the states in the Senate and to guarantee them "a republican form of government." In 1912, the Supreme Court was asked to declare an Oregon system of direct legislation through the initiative and referendum to be a violation of a republican, i.e., representative, form of government. However, the Court ruled that the enforcement of this provision lay with the Congress, and it has continued to refuse judicial interpretation or enforcement of this language.

INTERSTATE RELATIONS

The Constitution imposes certain obligations on the states in their relationships with each other. For one thing, they are required to extend the same privileges and immunities to citizens from other states that their own citizens enjoy. This means that out-of-state residents have the right to make contracts in the state, hold property, and have access to the courts, just as the state's own citizens.

However, the interstate privileges and immunities clause (Article IV, section 2) does not preclude a state from treating citizens of other states differently when there are acceptable reasons why the two groups should be placed on different footings. For example, the right to engage in normal businesses is protected, but the practice of such professions as medicine and law can be restricted to those licensed by the state. Similarly, a state can prevent persons coming from other states from voting until they have resided in the state for a certain period. Students from outside a state may be charged higher tuition in a state university than residents of the state.[1]

Another obligation is that each state must accord full faith and credit to

[1] But in *Vlandis v. Kline* (1973) the Supreme Court ruled that a Connecticut statute which required students admitted to state universities as nonresidents to pay nonresident tuition for their entire four years was held unconstitutional as a violation of due process. A Washington law requiring one year of residence in the state to qualify as a resident for tuition purposes was upheld in *Sturgis v. Washington* (1973).

the public acts, records, and judicial proceedings of every other state. Consequently a court judgment rendered in one state can, if properly authenticated, be enforced in another state. Divorces granted in one state are generally recognized in all other states, although the lenient divorce laws in such states as Nevada and Florida have created some problems. In a 1945 case, the Supreme Court held that North Carolina could refuse to recognize a Nevada divorce since it could be demonstrated that the parties, long-time residents of North Carolina, had never intended to establish a bona fide residence in Nevada.

The full faith and credit clause does not require a state to enforce the criminal laws of another state. The only obligation here is the provision requiring states to surrender fugitives from justice on the request of the governor of the state concerned. The Supreme Court has held that the federal government cannot force a state official to take such action, and governors occasionally do refuse to honor a request for extradition. However, most of the states have adopted a uniform criminal extradition act. Also, Congress has adopted a law making it a federal offense for a person to go from one state to another with the intent of avoiding prosecution or imprisonment.

The Constitution authorizes interstate compacts, through the rather negative device of forbidding such compacts unless Congress consents to them. Interstate compacts have been employed to deal with such regional problems as conservation of natural resources, sharing of water in interstate streams, flood and pollution control, and regulation of interstate river basins or harbors. For example, the Port of New York Authority was set up by the states of New York and New Jersey to develop and operate harbor and transportation facilities in the bistate area. Compacts have not, however, proved very successful in achieving regulatory purposes.

The states have also joined in a program of promoting uniform state laws through a national conference; and they have sought to achieve more general cooperative purposes through the Council of State Governments, a central secretariat that provides research, publication, and information services for the states. An annual Governors' Conference provides an opportunity for state executives to discuss common problems, and the governors also hold regional meetings.

THE POLITICS OF FEDERALISM

Whereas the constitutional arrangements thus far discussed provide the framework for operation of the federal system, the actual activities of and relationships between the federal and state governments at any particular period have been determined by the felt needs of the time, by popular demands and expectations as translated through the political process into governmental decisions. Looked at over the long reaches of United States history, there is an obvious trend toward increasing the powers and functions of the federal government. Yet it is safe to say that Washington has never yet used all the powers it might justifiably claim under the Constitution, and there have been periods when the centralizing trend was reversed. The central-local relationship has been the product of political conflict, compromise, and consensus.

No detailed account of the politics of American federalism can be attempted here. Merely to follow the ebb and flow of centralizing trends through the major periods of our history is difficult. Of course the adoption of the Constitution was in itself a major victory of those forces favoring a strong national government, a victory which the Federalist party consolidated during the succeeding years under the astute guidance of Alexander Hamilton. But the anti-Federalist, states' rights forces were quickly rallied by Thomas Jefferson into a coalition strong enough to win the presidency in 1800 and ultimately to destroy the Federalist party itself. Once in office, however, Jefferson's Democrats by no means moved to dismantle the federal establishment. In fact, Jefferson is particularly remembered for his bold move in purchasing the Louisiana Territory, in spite of his own expressed doubts about the constitutionality of such federal action.

After the defeat of 1800, Federalist and nationalist ideology was kept alive by Chief Justice John Marshall on the Supreme Court. From 1801 to 1835, he devoted his immense judicial skill to broadening the constitutional interpretations of federal power. His successor, Roger B. Taney, was of the opposite persuasion, and the years up to the Civil War saw the pendulum swing back toward state powers.

Out of the Civil War, the Republican party emerged as the nationalist voice of the industrial East and Middle West, and the Democratic party as the states' rights spokesman of the South. But the responsibility of government that came to the Democratic party with Woodrow Wilson's election in 1912 and the necessities of wartime organization laid the foundation for a reversal of party positions, which was fully consolidated by Franklin D. Roosevelt's New Deal. From 1932 to 1952, the general Republican position was critical of the centralization attending the government's depression, war, and cold-war programs. In 1952, a Republican president who took office pledged to reverse these centralizing tides. Although President Eisenhower did largely succeed in halting further increases in federal functions, his efforts to find services that might be discontinued or returned to the states were almost completely without result.

Under Presidents Kennedy and Johnson, the federal government assumed a variety of new responsibilities—aid to education, enforcement of the right to vote and to a fair trial, guarantee that access to public accommodations would not be denied on grounds of race, programs for cleaning up polluted rivers and air and beautifying highways, assistance to cities in maintaining effective systems of public transportation and rebuilding the slums, and many other "Great Society" activities. President Nixon ran on a program of reducing centralization in Washington, and he made some progress in this direction, particularly through his revenue sharing program. But he also found it necessary in 1971 to set up a national price control system in an effort to control inflation, and he proposed national assumption of the welfare burden and a national system of medical insurance.

What this experience suggests is that shifts of power toward the central government are not the result of political ideologies or conspiracies or Supreme Court decisions, but are caused rather by the inexorable pressures of wars, depressions, new means of communication, urbanization, industrialization, technology, and all the other factors that have shrunk the size of our world and created problems so large and so urgent that of necessity they are pushed up to the national level for handling.

COOPERATIVE FEDERALISM

Actually, it is highly misleading to talk about federal centralization as though everything the federal government does must be taken away from the states, or as though the only choice to be made is between federal or state activity. In fact, a great many of the functions of our present federal system are performed jointly by two or three levels of government. Nor is this a twentieth-century development. From the very beginnings of American federalism, there has been more sharing of governmental functions than is commonly realized. Even before the Constitution was adopted, the Northwest Ordinance of 1787 gave grants-in-aid to the states for the support of public schools. Early examples of federal-state administrative cooperation occurred in operation of the militia, law enforcement, court practices, conduct of elections, public health measures, pilot laws, and numerous other fields.

Today the list of cooperative federal-state-local activities is almost endless. In the public health field, federal, state, and local programs are so intertwined that it may be difficult for an official to know in what capacity he is operating at a particular time. The national network of highways has been built up under a federal-state cooperative program dating from 1916. The social security system, Selective Service, the National Guard—these and many other examples of cooperative federalism demonstrate how the levels of government work together.

Many of these joint efforts involve federal grants-in-aid to the states. Originally, federal grants were of land, but in the twentieth century they have been grants of federal funds. What are still called state "land-grant colleges" were originally established under the terms of the Morrill Act of 1862. Major grant-in-aid programs now cover the construction of highways and airports; elementary, secondary, and vocational education; social security programs; forest development; and law enforcement.

A congressional study in 1969 revealed a total of more than a thousand separate grant programs, of which 138 were of major significance. Highway construction has historically received the most federal funds; but in 1967 public assistance payments, primarily for welfare, moved into the top position. Grants for education increased sharply after passage of the Education Act of 1965. In 1969, it was estimated that 18 percent of all local revenues came from the federal government.

Grants are made available to the states in order to promote activities regarded by Congress as beneficial to the public welfare, which the states might not undertake without federal stimulus or support or which they might be unable to undertake or to perform effectively except as part of a general program. One of the arguments often made for the grant-in-aid system is that federal funds, which are distributed among the states according to a formula specified by Congress in each grant statute, can perform an equalizing function and enable the poorer states to bring their services up to an acceptable national minimum.

Another effect of the grant system has been to revitalize some areas of state activity and enable the states to retain certain programs that might otherwise have gone to the federal government by default. When federal grants are made available to the states, there are accompanying federal regulations and requirements that ensure that state administration of the program will meet federally established standards. The states, of course, are also required to match the federal funds in some degree.

Arguments against the grant system are that it limits state discretion in the spending of funds and forces the states to undertake programs simply because they will bring in federal money. Moreover, most grants specify in detail what local governments can spend for particular projects and tie local officials in a maze of federal regulations.

There are two alternatives to the traditional grant-in-aid. One is the block grant, which supplies money for a specified purpose but leaves the states free to allocate the funds within the purposes of that program. Block grants were provided by the Crime Control Act of 1968 for the programs of the Law Enforcement Assistance Administration. In 1974 the Housing and Community Development Act consolidated eight federal programs, including model cities and urban renewal, into one block grant of $11.2 billion over a three-year period.

The second alternative is revenue sharing, under which the federal government turns over lump sums to state and local governments with no limitations or directions as to the purposes for which they are to be spent. This plan was first proposed by the Council of Economic Advisors in the Johnson administration. President Nixon made revenue sharing the major plank in his domestic program and secured its adoption by Congress in 1972. The statute authorizes sharing $30.2 billion of federal revenues with state and local governments over a five-year period, one-third of each state's share going to the state government, and two-thirds going to local governments in the state. Allocation formulas take into account population, tax effort, and relative income.

Revenue sharing is understandably popular with state and local officials, and though authorized for only five years appears likely to be a permanent feature of federal-state relations. Nixon's case for revenue sharing was that it would take power out of Washington and return it to "the people." Many local governments have in fact responded by arranging for some popular participation in allocation of the annual grant.

But revenue sharing is not without its problems. The most serious objection is that it permits federal funds to be spent without national purpose or direction, and without any requirement of specific performance from recipients. Early experience showed that the states tended to use their money to pay bills, lower or hold down taxes, balance budgets, or avoid borrowing money. Cities were more likely to spend their money on new programs involving environmental protection, transportation, recreational facilities, and public safety. Relatively small amounts were allocated to the poor and the elderly. In addition, there is no reason why funds should go to some 38,000 units of government, some of which have neither demonstrated a need nor provided a use for the money, and the allocation formula fails to ensure that jurisdictions with the greatest need get the greatest assistance.

The federal government has experimented with a regional approach to problems that concern more than one state but not the entire country. The most notable example is the Tennessee Valley Authority, established by Congress in 1933 to develop the resources of the Tennessee River basin. The TVA is headed by an independent three-man board based in the area and entirely outside the Washington bureaucracy. This organization has built up a highly efficient power system and encouraged regional developments that have substantially improved living standards in the area.

THE FUTURE OF THE STATES

Questions about the proper distribution of functions between the federal government and the states will continue to arise. Centralizing trends will not be halted by revenue sharing or slogans about returning power to the people. The basic domestic problems of inflation, poverty, pollution, conservation, welfare, health care, housing, urban deterioration, transportation, and energy sources demand central attention. But that does not make the role of the states unimportant. There is no doubting the developing distaste for "big government," and the disillusionment with Washington resulting from Watergate. As the reputation of national institutions has declined, that of the states has tended to rise.

The reapportionment of state legislatures under Supreme Court decree made them more representative and more alert to the problems of their urban areas. A 1974 survey showed that the states, far from being mere road builders, were spending 40 percent of their revenues to support education, while another 25 percent went for welfare. From 1950 to 1970, the number of federal employees increased from 2.1 million to 2.9 million, but state employment rose at a considerably faster rate, from 1.2 million to 3.0 million. State fiscal systems have been made more equitable. In 1974 they were deriving 23 percent of their revenues from personal income taxes, compared with only 9 percent some 15 years earlier. By 1974 all 50 states had consumer protection programs and had made some provision for relief in property taxes for the aged and the poor. A dozen states had no-fault auto insurance, and a number were ahead of Congress in campaign reform legislation. By popular vote in 1972 California inaugurated the nation's most comprehensive land-use plan for its thousand-mile coastline. A 1974 poll showed that 60 percent of Americans thought their governor was doing a good job, at a time when the President was getting only a 25 percent rating.

The states have an essential place in American federalism. They have their shortcomings as rational administrative units, but they are viable social and cultural enclaves. Politically their status is firmly embedded in the composition of the Senate and in the major political parties, which at the national level are only coalitions of state organizations. They are valuable laboratories in which new kinds of legislation and new political movements can be tested. Vigorous and dynamic state governments are needed to relieve the centralizing pressures on Washington and to provide a healthy balance in the federal system.

REVIEW QUESTIONS

1 How did Hamilton and Jefferson disagree as to the powers of Congress?

2 What is the doctrine of dual federalism?

3 How are conflicts between federal and state statutes handled?

4 What is the importance of the Supreme Court's power to review state court decisions?

5 What is the difference between the doctrines of interposition and nullification?

6 How can a state treat out-of-state residents differently from its own citizens without violating the interstate privileges and immunities clause?

7 What are the problems in according full faith and credit to Nevada divorces?

8 For what purposes have interstate compacts been used?

9 What are the advantages and disadvantages of federal grants-in-aid to the states?

10 What is the difference between block grants and revenue sharing?

3 CONGRESS AND FEDERAL POWERS

The Constitution sets up American governmental institutions on the separation-of-powers principle; and legislative, executive, and judicial functions are entrusted to three separate branches of government. The executive and the legislative are independent of each other in that they are each elected by separate electoral processes for assured terms of office. The President cannot dissolve Congress or shorten its term or remove any of its members. The Congress, even though it may have a majority that does not support the President, cannot remove him from office except by the difficult and politically dangerous process of impeachment. The federal judiciary, although appointed by the President and confirmed by the Senate, is independent in the sense that it has tenure for life; and its authority to enforce constitutional requirements on both the President and Congress is universally accepted.

Thus the term "separation of powers" has a degree of validity in describing the American system when contrasted with, for example, the English plan of concentrating authority in the legislature. The English executive is a council of ministers, headed by the Prime Minister, which is in effect a committee of the majority party in the House of Commons. The English judiciary has great prestige and security, but it cannot challenge the legitimacy of parliamentary action.

In many respects, however, "separation of powers" is a most misleading description of the American government. More accurately, the United States Constitution provides for a government of *separated institutions sharing powers*. The process of government requires that these separate institutions work together with some measure of effective cooperation, and this is perhaps the key problem of the constitutional system of the United States.

THE SEPARATED INSTITUTIONS

The institutional separation between Congress and the executive is exaggerated by their diverse electoral bases. The Senate is composed of two members from every state elected for six-year terms; it overrepresents the smaller states. In the House, a 435-man body whose members are apportioned to the states on the basis of population, the representatives are elected from congressional districts for two-year terms. The House represents local interests, particularly those of the rural areas, which until recently have had more seats than they deserved on a population basis. The President, as will be discussed more fully in the next chapter, is chosen by an electoral system that gives disproportionate weight to the votes of the large industrial states. Thus each of these separated institutions has its own constituency.

Congress and the executive are, it is true, linked to some degree by a device for which the Constitution made no provision, the political party. However, there are many reasons why parties are of limited effectiveness in achieving cooperation between Congress and the President.[1] The main problem is that American national parties are federations of state and local organizations, which join their efforts every four years to nominate and elect a President but which otherwise tend to go their separate ways. There is little national party discipline, and the members of Congress are more likely to win elections through attention to the interests of their state or district than through the help of the national party. Within each party there is a wide range of political views, and any President will find that a substantial number of his party's legislators disagree with his general policy position.

There are other factors limiting the effectiveness of party as a bridge between Congress and President. The electoral system does not guarantee that the President will have a majority of his own party in both houses of Congress or even in one house. Though a President usually starts each four-year term with a majority in Congress, the mid-term legislative elections two years later customarily reduce his party's membership in Congress. President Eisenhower confronted Democratic majorities in both houses of Congress during six of his eight years in office, and President Nixon had to deal with Democratic majorities in both houses during his entire Presidency.

Even when the President's party is in control of Congress, the legislative leadership may not be particularly hospitable to the President's views. The selection of House and Senate leaders is decided by the legislators themselves, and presidential interference in favor of his own candidates would be resented. Again, the chairmen of committees are generally selected on the basis of seniority, which means that legislators unfriendly to the administration program may be in key congressional posts.

Separated by constitutional provisions on election and tenure, representing different constituencies of voters, and inadequately coordinated by party, the President and Congress are rivals for power; and their characteristic relation is one of tension. This state is not a symptom of governmental failure. It is rather an indication that the system of separation of powers is operating normally. The Congress is too numerous and too poorly organized to originate a legislative program, or to assume leadership functions. That is the executive role. The President must tell Congress what he wants to have done. Congress, jealous of its autonomy, does not like to be told; and it usually revises, delays, or ignores the

---

[1] For a fuller discussion, see *Politics and Voters* by Hugh A. Bone and Austin Ranney, in this series.

President's program. A popular President, using press conferences and television, patronage and persuasion, can usually get his way in the end. During the first hundred days of Roosevelt's New Deal, Congress was so acquiescent that it was called a rubber stamp; and Eisenhower, with the help of the majority leader in the Senate, Lyndon Johnson, got along well with a Democratic Congress. On the other hand, Nixon's operation of the Presidency on a quasi-imperial basis disposed him toward a policy of ignoring or coercing Congress rather than seeking cooperation, and was a major factor in his downfall.

LAWMAKING

The Constitution vests "all legislative powers herein granted" in the Congress. But lawmaking is one of the many "shared functions" in the constitutional system of the United States. The President is an indispensable participant, either by constitutional provision or by custom and necessity, in all stages of this process. In recent decades, practically all important legislative proposals have originated in the executive. Article II, section 3, provides that the President "shall from time to time give to the Congress information of the state of the Union, and recommend to their consideration such measures as he shall judge necessary and expedient." Accordingly, the State of the Union message with a proposed legislative program is submitted by the President to Congress at the beginning of each regular session. It is followed by the President's budget message transmitting the executive expenditure recommendations for the following year and the President's report on the state of the national economy as required by the Full Employment Act of 1946.

While Congress is in session, the policy leadership of the administration is continuously manifested in the preparation of draft bills, testimony before congressional committees by department heads and other officials of the executive branch, and use of the President's vast powers as party leader and manipulator of public opinion. Under Article II, section 3, the President may call Congress into special session to consider legislation he wants adopted, a power he has often used to bring added pressure on Congress.

All legislation must be submitted to the President for his signature before it becomes effective. Congress can override a presidential veto only by an extraordinary two-thirds majority in both houses. The President can permit a bill to become law without his signature by failing to sign and return it within 10 days after he has received it. This procedure is used when the President does not approve of a bill, but feels it impossible or impolitic to veto it. However, in these circumstances the bill will become law only if Congress is still in session after the 10 days have expired. If Congress adjourns within the 10-day period, the bill does not become law, and is said to have been given a "pocket veto."[2]

[2] In 1973 a federal court of appeals ruled that a congressional Christmas recess did not constitute an "adjournment" in the constitutional sense, and consequently did not justify a pocket veto.

The President must accept or reject a bill in toto; he has no power to veto items in a bill. Thus there is a temptation for Congress to attach legislation that the President is known to oppose as a "rider" to some vitally important bill. Numerous proposals to give the President an "item veto" (i.e., the power to veto particular items without vetoing the entire bill), primarily with respect to appropriations measures, have uniformly failed.

In two particular fields of lawmaking—control of finances and departmental organization—Congress has gone far toward yielding its control to the President. The Budget and Accounting Act of 1921 established the principle and practice of the executive budget, under which the President is responsible for formulating and presenting to Congress a complete, detailed expenditure plan for the following fiscal year. Congress retains authority, in enacting the annual appropriation acts, to modify the executive budget in any way it sees fit. But as a practical matter, the congressional appropriations committees can give only a limited review to expenditure proposals totaling more than $300 billion annually.

A congressional appropriation has generally been regarded by the executive as merely an authorization to spend. Consequently, Presidents have on numerous occasions—when Congress had appropriated funds for purposes or in amounts which they did not approve—placed part of the appropriation in "reserves" or "impounded" some or all of the funds. Minor controversies between the two branches resulted, but it was not until President Nixon undertook to impound appropriated funds on a massive scale that the issue reached constitutional proportions. He not only made deep cuts in many domestic programs but even terminated congressionally approved operations by a total impoundment of their appropriations. During Nixon's first term impounded funds amounted to at least $15 billion and for fiscal year 1974, $11.8 billion. The usual targets were appropriations for highway construction, housing, control of water pollution, and other environmental programs, and the usual justification was the need to hold down expenditures to control inflation.

Intended recipients of these grants quickly took the administration to court and were generally successful. The state of Missouri, for example, won a court of appeals decision requiring release of highway trust funds allotted to that state. The Supreme Court in *Train v. City of New York* (1975) held that the language of the federal water pollution control act permitted no impounding and ordered the allocation of all funds authorized by the act.

Congress, seeing in presidential impoundment a denial of its power to spend, make laws, and override vetoes, undertook to develop legislation that would drastically reduce the opportunity for presidential intervention. At the same time Congress recognized that its own slipshod fiscal practices, which never required appropriations to be considered in relation to anticipated revenues, had furnished the President with justification for his actions. Consequently a serious effort was undertaken to reform congressional budget procedures, which resulted in the Budget Reform Act of 1974. Briefly, the act creates budget committees in each house to oversee expenditures and revenues and establishes a congressional budget office to give Congress the type of expertise now available to the President through his Office of Management and Budget. The act also provides procedures by which Congress can force the President to spend funds he has impounded.

Congress has power to pass laws setting up the federal departments and agencies, but since 1933 it has delegated considerable responsibility for federal reorganization to the President. A series of reorganization acts have authorized the President to prepare "reorganization plans," which may set up new departments or transfer bureaus or functions from one agency to another. These plans are submitted to Congress, and then go into effect automatically unless vetoed by either house of Congress within a specified time period. President Eisenhower created the Department of Health, Education, and Welfare in this manner in 1953. President Kennedy's reorganization plan establishing a Department of Urban Affairs was vetoed by the House in 1962; but in 1965 Congress acceded to President Johnson's request and created by statute a department with somewhat more limited powers, the Department of Housing and Urban Development. President Nixon replaced the Bureau of the Budget with an expanded Office of Management and Budget by his reorganization plan of 1970.

INVESTIGATORY POWER

In an examination of the more significant legislative powers, the first to be noted is not even mentioned in the Constitution. The power of Congress to investigate is an implied power, supplementary to its specifically assigned functions to legislate, to appropriate, to pass on the elections and returns of members, and so on. It is an extremely broad power, because the need of Congress for information is broad, but at the same time it is not free from constitutional limitations.

The instrument through which Congress brings pressure on witnesses before its committees is the power to punish refusal to testify as contempt of Congress. Although Congress can itself try persons for contempt of its authority and imprison those found guilty, it has preferred to act through the courts. By an 1857 statute, Congress provided that persons refusing to appear before a legislative committee or to answer questions pertinent to an inquiry should be deemed guilty of a misdemeanor and be subject to indictment and judicial punishment. Under this act, there is full opportunity for reviewing courts to determine whether the legislative conclusion that contempt had been committed was justified.

The Communist-hunting activities of the House Committee on Un-American Activities and Senator Joseph McCarthy's activities in the Committee on Government Operations between 1950 and 1954 posed some difficult questions concerning the scope of the investigatory power. Many persons refused to answer inquiries by these committees on the ground that under the Fifth Amendment they could not be forced to give information that might be used against them in a criminal prosecution. This course guaranteed against a contempt citation but laid the witness open to loss of employment and reputation, as witness Senator McCarthy's frequent charges about "Fifth Amendment Communists." Other witnesses refused to take refuge in the Fifth Amendment and declined to answer on the claim that their rights to freedom of speech and opinion under the First Amendment were being infringed.

For a considerable period, the Supreme Court avoided passing on the serious constitutional issues raised by these inquiries. Finally, in *Watkins v. United States* (1957), the Court did uphold a witness who had declined to testify before the Un-American Activities Committee and indicated some intention to assume a measure of responsibility for determining whether congressional committees were operating within their constitutional authority. "There is no congressional power to expose for the sake of exposure," wrote Chief Justice Warren.

The *Watkins* decision was bitterly criticized as an infringement on congressional freedom to secure information, though in fact it resulted in no revision of the authority under which the Un-American Activities Committee operated and little change in its procedures. Then, two years later, the Court by a 5 to 4 vote substantially reversed the *Watkins* holding in *Barenblatt v. United States* (1959). Here the Court decided that the congressional concern for preservation of the country must override the First Amendment rights of individuals. Justice John Marshall Harlan added that the Court could not look into the "motives" of congressional investigators. While the Court thus declined to question the scope of the investigatory power, it did become increasingly concerned about the procedural rights of witnesses before congressional committees; and it reversed contempt convictions in a substantial number of cases on these grounds.

The investigation by the Senate Select Committee on Watergate, under the chairmanship of Senator Sam Ervin, was a television spectacular during the spring and summer of 1973. It provided a forum for substantiating former White House counsel John Dean's charges connecting Nixon to the Watergate cover-up and revealed the existence of the famous tapes which ultimately led to the Nixon resignation. The efforts of the committee to secure a number of the tapes were frustrated by court rulings, however, and in its later stages the committee was largely eclipsed by the impeachment investigation conducted by the House Judiciary Committee and by various court proceedings against principals in the Watergate affair.

THE POWER TO IMPEACH

Congress possesses the power to impeach the President or any other administrative or judicial officer. The impeachment procedure involves both houses of Congress, the House of Representatives serving as the indicting body by voting impeachment resolutions. These charges are then tried before the Senate, with the Chief Justice presiding if the President is on trial. A two-thirds vote of the Senate is necessary for conviction. Ten federal judges have been impeached, of whom four were convicted. Three other officials have been impeached—a senator, a cabinet member, and President Andrew Johnson—none of whom was convicted.

The failure of the Senate, by one vote, to convict Johnson, and the vindictive partisanship responsible for his impeachment, were generally thought to have so discredited the impeachment device as to preclude its future use against a President. Consequently, as the possible implication of President Nixon in the Watergate scandals began to emerge, initial suggestions of impeachment were not taken seriously. But after the shattering disclosures before the Ervin committee, Nixon's initial refusal to surrender tapes subpoenaed by Judge John J. Sirica for Watergate trials, and the "Saturday night massacre" which saw the firing of Special Prosecutor Archibald Cox for refusing to stop his efforts to get the tapes and the consequent resignations of Attorney General Elliott Richardson and Assistant Attorney General William D. Ruckelshaus for their refusal to carry out the firing order—the situation changed. In October, 1973, an impeachment inquiry was begun by the House Judiciary Committee, under the chairmanship of Peter W. Rodino.

Two major constitutional issues were raised by these proceedings. One was the meaning of the constitutional language in Article II, section 4, providing impeachment for "treason, bribery, or other high crimes and misdemeanors." For the President it was argued that impeachment is limited to serious, indictable crimes. The contrary position, based on English parliamentary practice (where the phrase "high crimes and misdemeanors" originated) and various statements of the Founding Fathers, was that impeachment was intended as a remedy for serious abuse of executive power.

A second issue was whether there was any limit on the investigative powers of the House Judiciary Committee when conducting an impeachment inquiry. The argument for the committee was that the impeachment power of Congress is an intentional breach in the separation of powers principle, and that consequently Congress is the sole judge of what evidence is relevant and can compel its production by the executive. The President's position was that preservation of the integrity of the Presidency required that he decide what evidence was relevant to the investigation, and in fact he refused to obey subpoenas for tapes demanded by the committee. However, the committee was able to secure some tapes that had been submitted to Judge Sirica, and on April 30, 1974, Nixon released to the public edited versions of a number of tapes.

After lengthy preparation by its staff and several months of closed briefings and hearings, the Judiciary Committee, in televised sessions in July, 1974, voted three articles of impeachment against President Nixon. The first, charging obstruction of justice by the Watergate cover-up, was adopted by a vote of 27 to 11, with 6 Republicans joining the 21 Democrats. The second alleged abuse of presidential power by misuse of the FBI, the CIA, and other government agencies; it was adopted by a vote of 28 to 10. The third, charging Nixon with contempt of Congress by refusing to obey the committee's subpoenas, was more narrowly passed by 21 to 17. The committee refused to approve two additional articles dealing with Nixon's taxes and the secret bombing of Cambodia.

Ten Republicans supported the President in the votes on all three adopted articles. Their position generally was that, while many unlawful acts had admittedly occurred, Nixon's responsibility for them had not been proved. They wanted evidence as strong as a "smoking gun" before they would charge the President with high crimes and misdemeanors. That evidence was supplied when on August 5, under pressure of the Supreme Court's unanimous opinion, Nixon released transcripts of tapes revealing that he had taken command of the cover-up only six days after the Watergate break-in, and that he had kept this information from his staff and his counsel. With an obstruction of justice thus established by the President's own words, sentiment in Congress and the country, already unfavorable to the President, turned overwhelmingly for impeachment. But that would require several more months, and there was even greater demand for an immediate termination of the crisis by resignation. After resisting for several days, Nixon resigned effective August 9, 1974, the first American President to leave office by resignation.

THE TAXING POWER

The broadest grant of fiscal authority to Congress is that in Article I, section 8, clause 1: "The Congress shall have power to lay and collect taxes, duties, imposts and excises, to pay the debts and provide for the common defence and general welfare of the United States." While this very broad grant of power is limited by some specific provisions, appearing elsewhere in Article I, the only restriction to give serious trouble has been the ban on "direct" taxes unless levied in proportion to population. The federal income tax adopted by Congress in 1894 was held to be a direct tax and so unconstitutional. This decision delayed the inauguration of income taxation until 1913, when the Sixteenth Amendment was adopted.

The Supreme Court has been asked on occasion to develop additional limitations on the taxing power, but only very rarely has it done so. Questions have been raised about the right of Congress to use the taxing power for purposes other than raising revenue. The best example is the protective tariff, which may impose customs duties so high as to keep particular foreign goods out of the country altogether. The purpose of such rates is not to bring in revenue but to protect American manufacturers from foreign competition. The first tariff law was passed in 1789, but the Supreme Court never had occasion to rule on the constitutionality of this form of taxation until 1928. Then the Court upheld the tariff laws, saying: "So long as the motive of Congress and the effect of its legislative action are to secure revenue for the benefit of the general government, the existence of other motives in the selection of taxes can not invalidate Congressional action."

The Court has tended to use similar rationalizations to justify other tax statutes possessing obvious regulatory features. In 1866, Congress imposed a 10 percent tax on notes issued by state banks, for the clear purpose of driving such notes out of circulation in favor of the notes of national banks. The Court upheld this action in 1869 on the ground that the taxing power was being used merely to aid the national government in its admitted power to establish a sound and uniform currency. An even more extreme use of federal taxing power was a tax of 10 cents a pound on colored oleomargarine, while uncolored butter substitutes were taxed only ¼ cent per pound. This tax was obviously passed at the behest of the dairy interests, but the Court denied in *McCray v. United States* (1904) that "the motives or purposes of Congress are open to judicial inquiry in considering the power of that body."

There have been a few tax programs, however, in which the Court did find congressional nonrevenue motives too apparent to accept. One was the child labor tax, adopted in 1919 after the first child labor act, based on the commerce clause, had been held unconstitutional. The tax statute was clumsily drafted; and the Court found its regulatory purpose plainly visible on the face of the statute, with no need to go behind the act to prove that it was not a revenue measure. Similarly a grossly disproportional federal excise tax, amounting to $1,000, imposed only on retail liquor dealers carrying on business in violation of local law, was declared unconstitutional.

A second limitation which the Court has read into the federal taxing power is an immunity for the operations and activities of state and local governments. The immunity doctrine was first developed by the Court in *McCulloch v. Maryland* (1819), when it served to protect the Bank of the United States from state taxation. It was not until 1871 that this doctrine was applied in reverse to hold the salary of a state judge immune from the temporary federal Civil War income tax. In 1895, the *Pollock* decision exempted from federal taxation the interest on state and local bonds.

From this start, the conservative Court of the 1920s went on to extend tax immunity to a wide variety of state-connected activities. For example, a federal tax on the income that private persons derived from leasing state-owned oil lands was invalidated by the Court. During the same period, federal immunity from state taxation was similarly expanded by the Court.

These exaggerated notions of intergovernmental tax immunity were eliminated by the more liberal Court of the late 1930s. Reciprocal exemption of both federal and state employees from income taxation was terminated, and the oil-lands leasing cases were reversed. Tax exemption on income from state and municipal bonds remained as the principal limitation on congressional taxing power, and even this exemption probably no longer rests on a constitutional base.

Federal tax statutes have occasionally been held to conflict with constitutional guarantees. A federal tax on persons engaged in the illegal business of gambling was held in 1968 to compel self-incrimination, and in 1969 the same conclusion was reached as to the federal marijuana transfer tax act which required that the names of all persons paying the tax be turned over to law enforcement authorities.

SPENDING AND BORROWING

The language of Article I, section 8, authorizes Congress to levy taxes in order to "pay the debts and provide for the common defence and general welfare." This is spending authority of such expansiveness as to leave Congress substantially free from limitations on its appropriating power. The principal tests have occurred in connection with federal grant-in-aid legislation under which Congress has made federal funds available to the states for financing programs that Congress wishes to promote.

The first important effort to invalidate such a federal spending program came in *Massachusetts v. Mellon* (1923), involving the Maternity Act of 1921, which offered funds to the states for carrying on programs of health protection for mothers and infants. But this attack was frustrated by the Court's ruling that a lawsuit challenging the validity of a federal spending program can be prosecuted only by a litigant who has a sufficient legal interest in federal expenditures to give him standing to sue. Neither the state of Massachusetts nor an individual federal income taxpayer had sufficient standing to entitle them to raise the issue, the Court held.

In spite of that ruling, the peculiar circumstances of *United States v. Butler* (1936) did make it possible for the Supreme Court in that case to strike down an exercise of federal spending power. The Agricultural Adjustment Act of 1933 had provided for federal payments to farmers cooperating in the government's program of price stabilization through production control. The money paid the farmers was to come from processing taxes on agricultural commodities authorized by the same statute. This statutory joinder of a spending program with the tax arrangements for financing it was quite unusual and gave the Court, which was at that time in a bitterly anti-New Deal mood, an opening that it quickly exploited. It held that the tax and the spending were in fact "parts of a single scheme" to regulate and control agricultural production, a field that belonged to the states. Consequently, the act was unconstitutional under the Tenth Amendment. However, the Court in 1937 refused to invalidate the tax provisions of the Social Security Act on similar grounds.

Pressure on the Supreme Court to review the massive educational grants provided under the Elementary and Secondary Education Act of 1965 finally led to the partial overruling of *Massachusetts v. Mellon*. Because of the assistance these grants indirectly provided for parochial schools, there were serious charges that the statute amounted to an establishment of religion. On *Flast v. Cohen* (1968), the Supreme Court agreed that First Amendment questions of this gravity could be raised by taxpayers' suits in the federal courts.

Congress has constitutionally unlimited power "to borrow money on the credit of the United States." There is no specific authority to issue paper money, and the "greenbacks" by which the Civil War was financed were first held unconstitutional in 1870 by a 4 to 3 vote of the Supreme Court. However, after two vacancies on the Court had been filled by President Ulysses S. Grant, the Court reconsidered the issue and overruled the first decision by a vote of 5 to 4.

In 1933, the New Deal reduced the gold content of the dollar and nullified all provisions in private contracts and government bonds that called for payment in gold. The Supreme Court upheld this action as applied to private contracts, on the ground that individuals could not be allowed to frustrate the government's monetary program. The government itself could not, on the other hand, abrogate the promise to pay in gold coin, but the Court kept this holding from having any practical effect by adding that suit could be brought only for actual losses as a result of the government's action. Congress terminated the matter by passing a statute denying consent to sue the government on these grounds.

THE COMMERCE POWER

"The Congress shall have power," says Article I, section 8, clause 3, "to regulate commerce with foreign nations, and among the several states, and with the Indian tribes." The language is in terms of a positive grant of power to Congress, but in fact its purpose was also to take away from the states this power which they had so seriously abused to the detriment of general commercial development under the Articles of Confederation. As it turned out, Congress was slow to utilize this grant of authority, and for the first century of national existence the primary problem in interpreting the commerce clause was to decide how much regulatory power remained with the states under the Constitution.

This was the issue presented in *Gibbons v. Ogden* (1824), the first commerce clause decision and one in which Chief Justice Marshall laid down principles that have affected all subsequent interpretations of the constitutional language. New York State had granted to certain interests a monopoly on steamboat transportation on waters within the state. The monopoly was challenged by Thomas Gibbons, who was operating a steamboat between New York and New Jersey under a license granted by the federal government; and the Court struck down the New York monopoly on a finding of conflict between the state and federal statutes.

In the course of the decision, Marshall expressed the opinion that the congressional power over commerce "may very well be restricted to that commerce which concerns more states than one." Eventually this suggestion was developed into the distinction between "interstate" and "intrastate" commerce, and federal power was limited to the former category.

Any operation that crosses a state line obviously falls in the "interstate" area. Thus interstate railroad, motor, aviation, pipeline, navigation, electric, or communications services are clearly subject to congressional control. Conversely, commercial operations that do not cross state lines have a prima facie claim to escape congressional regulation. This constitutional distinction came to be of great practical importance toward the end of the nineteenth century when Congress began to make important use of its regulatory powers by such laws as the interstate Commerce Act and the Sherman Antitrust Act. Thus a prosecution of the sugar trust under the Sherman Act was defeated by the Supreme Court in 1895 on the ground that the refining of sugar took place in one state and was a completely separate process from its distribution in interstate commerce. "Commerce succeeds to manufacture, and is not a part of it," the Court said.

Over "commerce" as thus interpreted, however, the Supreme Court has approved complete exercise of congressional power to accomplish not only protection and promotion but also restriction or even complete prohibition. In fact, Congress has on numerous occasions used the com-

merce power as a kind of national police power. A statute making it unlawful to transport lottery tickets from state to state was upheld by the Court
in 1903, and the same device of exclusion from the channels of interstate
commerce was later successfully used against impure food and drugs and
the white slave traffic.

Congress then sought to use this same method to attack child labor by
statute in 1916, but the Court held the act unconstitutional by a 5 to 4 vote
in the famous case of *Hammer v. Dagenhart* (1918). The Court tried to
explain this inconsistency by arguing that lottery tickets and impure foods
were harmful in and of themselves, whereas goods produced by child
labor "are of themselves harmless." It was obvious from the beginning
that this distinction was irrelevant to a determination of congressional
power, and the decision was overruled by the Supreme Court in 1941.

The commerce concept has never depended entirely on the test of
crossing a state line, however. After all, Marshall had talked about commerce that "concerns" more than one state, and commerce need not
cross a state line to be of concern to other states or to the nation. The
Supreme Court has long held that commercial transactions taking place
entirely within a state may have such an effect on commerce among the
states as to justify or require their regulation.

This "effect" doctrine has been applied in many situations. For example, where there is a "stream of commerce" moving across state lines, as
in the raising of cattle and sending them off to stockyards to be slaugh-
tered and prepared as meat products or in the growing, transportation,
and distribution of grain, sales in the stockyards or on the grain ex-
changes are integral parts of a stream of commerce which are subject to
congressional regulation. Again, where intrastate freight rates provide unfair competition with goods moving under interstate rates, then Congress
can control the intrastate rates.

The "effect" doctrine has the potentiality, if liberally interpreted, of extending congressional control to all commerce, for there is no commercial
transaction that does not have some slight effect on the national economy. The Supreme Court was well aware of this possibility, and so it
endeavored to provide some restrictions to keep the effect doctrine within
bounds. The device developed for this purpose was the "direct-indirect"
distinction. A direct effect on commerce could be the basis for federal
control, but an indirect effect could not. It was up to the Supreme Court, of
course, to decide which effects were direct and which indirect.

Perhaps the two most noteworthy cases in which the Court denied
Congress power to regulate because of this test were *Schechter Poultry
Corp. v. United States* (1935) and *Carter v. Carter Coal Co.* (1936). Two
important New Deal recovery statutes were invalidated by these decisions.

Under the National Recovery Act, the President had promulgated codes
of fair practice, fixing minimum wages and maximum hours and regulating
unfair or destructive competitive practices. In the *Schechter* case, the live
poultry code had been applied to a Brooklyn slaughtering plant that sold
chickens to retail dealers in the vicinity. The Court unanimously held that
these activities were not transactions in interstate commerce, nor could it
find that they directly affected commerce. Chief Justice Charles E.
Hughes was not able to define the difference between direct and indirect

effects, but he was sure that the distinction was a "fundamental one, essential to the maintenance of our constitutional system."

In the *Carter* case, the Court majority similarly concluded that, although interstate commerce might be "greatly" affected by the ills which the coal code was attempting to rememdy, it could never be "directly" affected. Coal production was a local activity. A production crisis in every part of the country simultaneously could never add up to a national problem with which Congress could deal.

A constitutional doctrine that held Congress powerless to alleviate national economic emergencies could not long be maintained. In 1937, in the landmark case of *National Labor Relations Board v. Jones & Laughlin Corp.*, the Court upheld the Wagner Act and in the process effectively terminated the "directness" test as a means of determining congressional power over commerce. In restoring what he called a "practical conception" of interstate commerce, Chief Justice Hughes did not overrule the *Schechter* and *Carter* opinions, but he said as little about them as was feasible. Speaking of the far-flung activities of this major steel company, he said:

> When industries organize themselves on a national scale, making their relation to interstate commerce the dominant factor in their activities, how can it be maintained that their industrial labor relations constitute a forbidden field into which Congress may not enter when it is necessary to protect interstate commerce from the paralyzing consequences of industrial war?

The *Jones & Laughlin* decision stated such a broad basis for the commerce power that few serious questions about the constitutional scope of congressional authority over commerce have subsequently arisen. The Fair Labor Standards Act, legislating minimum wages and maximum hours as conditions for the shipment of goods in interstate commerce, was upheld unanimously in 1941 in *United States v. Darby Lumber Co.*

Drastic agricultural regulations were accepted by the Court in *Wickard v. Filburn* (1942). Here a farmer raising 23 acres of wheat, none of it intended for interstate commerce since all was to be consumed on the farm or fed to stock, was held to have such an effect on interstate commerce as to be liable to marketing quotas fixed under an act of 1938. The Sherman Act was held applicable to the insurance business in 1944, ending an immunity from federal control that had been originally established by the Court in 1869. Professional baseball was given an illogical exemption from congressional regulation by the Supreme Court in 1922, an exemption continued in *Toolson v. New York Yankees* (1953) and *Flood v. Kuhn* (1972), although professional football and boxing were held to be subject to the Sherman Act.

As a result of the decisions since 1937, it is now clear that, in the words of Justice Benjamin N. Cardozo, the commerce power of Congress is "as broad as the need that evokes it." The most recent demonstration of this fact is the Civil Rights Act of 1964, in which Congress utilized the commerce power to forbid operators of restaurants, hotels, and other public accommodations to exclude persons on the ground of race. The theory of the act was that such discrimination was a burden on commerce and travelers, and the Supreme Court unanimously upheld the act in *Heart of Atlanta Motel v. United States* (1964). That the Commerce power could be used to restrict as well as to promote civil rights was demonstrated when Congress, incensed by peripatetic "black power" agitators, passed the Anti-Riot Act of 1968 punishing anyone who traveled in interstate commerce with the intent to incite or participate in a riot.

SUMMARY

From this review it is apparent that the Constitution gave Congress all the powers needed by a strong national government. The vast expansion of federal activities in the twentieth century has been achieved with only one change in the Constitution—the adoption of the income tax amendment, which made possible the financing of government on its present scale. Even the barrier against the income tax was erected, not by the Constitution, but by a highly questionable Supreme Court decision. Similarly the Court in a few decisions misinterpreted the broad language of the commerce clause, and for a time in 1935 and 1936 threatened to hamstring legislative power over the national economy. But this threat quickly passed as the Court returned to Marshall's principles.

Congress has all the power it needs to deal effectively with spaceage problems. If it has not always done so, the fault lies with legislative organization and leadership, not with lack of constitutional power.

REVIEW QUESTIONS

1 Is "separation of powers" an accurate phrase for describing the American governmental system?

2 Why does Congress have such a wide range of functions?

3 What are the main problems in executive-legislative cooperation?

4 How does the impeachment process operate?

5 What were the principal issues raised in the Nixon impeachment proceedings?

6 Why has the Supreme Court seemed reluctant to limit the investigatory power of Congress?

7 Can Congress use its taxing power to achieve purposes other than the raising of revenue?

8 What are the problems in testing the constitutionality of congressional spending?

9 What tests of congressional power to regulate commerce has the Supreme Court employed?

10 Is "intrastate" commerce ever subject to congressional regulation?

4 THE PRESIDENT

The establishment of a strong executive was one of the surprises of the Constitutional Convention. During the period immediately preceding the Revolution, the executive power, represented by the royal governors, had been far from popular, and when control passed into the hands of the states the first impulse was to slash away at the executive and exalt the legislatures. This same distrust of the executive was also present at Philadelphia in 1787, and proposals were heard that the executive branch be headed by a committee of three, for fear that a single official might develop monarchical powers. Again, it was argued that if a single executive was set up, he should be encumbered by a council.

These views were defeated by those who had seen the fumbling and the weakness of a headless government under the Articles of Confederation. Experience in the states had shown that an unchecked legislature could be as dangerous as a tyrannical executive ("The legislative department is everywhere extending the sphere of its activity," said Madison in 1787, "and drawing all power into its impetuous vortex"), and consequently a strong executive was favored to checkmate possible legislative usurpation. The office thus created has become the most important executive of a democratic country on the globe.

THE EXECUTIVE ROLE

The President gets his tremendous authority from a variety of sources. Of course the basic authorizations are in the Constitution itself. Article II begins: "The executive power shall be vested in a President of the United States of America." It then continues with a number of more or less specific provisions, such as the power to grant pardons, to receive ambassadors, to make appointments, and to see that the laws are faithfully executed. But the actual use of executive power under these authorizations varies greatly with different incumbents of the Presidency. The language of Article II was the same under Buchanan and Coolidge as it was under Lincoln and Franklin D. Roosevelt, but the results were far different. The potentialities of leadership in the executive office that a strong man or perilous times can develop have been demonstrated time and again in American history.

In part, the power of the American Presidency derives from the very character of the executive function, which John Locke referred to as "residual." Unlike the legislature, the executive is always in session, always capable of formulating a program and rousing opinion and so always available to fill in gaps and meet emergencies. In the ultimate emergency of war, these executive qualities combine with the constitutionally delegated role of Commander in Chief to produce an office of almost unlimited power.

The President's executive position is greatly strengthened by the method of his selection. While there are complications to be examined shortly, he is in effect chosen directly by the entire American electorate, and he is the only elected official (other than the Vice President) who has the entire nation for his constituency and the consequent responsibility of speaking for the national interest. In addition, the President is, by the fact of his election, the leader of his party—a source of great influence which the Constitution did not even contemplate.

Finally, the President is the ceremonial head of the nation, and his wife is the First Lady of the land. The good will that he may earn in performing his symbolic and nonpartisan duties can build up for him credit in the bank of public opinion on which he can draw in promoting his policy programs.

THE LIMITS OF EXECUTIVE POWER

With so many sources of authority on which he can rely, a resourceful President should have little difficulty in finding constitutional methods for achieving his purposes. The limitations on executive power that Presidents encounter are rarely the boundaries of the Constitution but rather the confines of political feasibility. As suggested in the preceding chapter, the President is under the constant pressure of Congress, which by the rules of the game must be suspicious of, if not hostile toward, many executive proposals or actions. Where joint action is required by the Constitution, the President is limited to what he can persuade Congress to accept.

Conflicts between the Supreme Court and the President have been less frequent, and generally the Court has recognized the right of the executive to exercise broad powers free from judicial control. In the early case of *Mississippi v. Johnson* (1867), the Court rejected a state suit seeking to restrain President Johnson from enforcing certain Reconstruction statutes, relying on "the general principles which forbid judicial interference with the exercise of Executive discretion."

An important continuing issue with respect to the legitimacy of presidential action has been the latitude which the President may claim in dealing with crises by using powers not specified in the Constitution. Does the President have "inherent" powers which he can exercise under emergency conditions?

In general, there have been two views on this subject. One is well summarized in the "stewardship" conception of the presidential office asserted by Theodore Roosevelt. In his *Autobiography* he set forth his belief "that it was not only his right but his duty to do anything that the needs of the Nation demanded unless such action was forbidden by the Constitution or by the laws."

On the other hand, William Howard Taft took a much more cautious and limited view of the President's powers. The President's proper role was faithfully to execute the *laws,* not his own conception of the national needs. In lectures which he gave in 1916 after his presidential term, he said:

> The true view of the Executive function is, as I conceive it, that the President can exercise no power which cannot be fairly and reasonably traced to some specific grant of power or justly implied and included within such express grant as proper and necessary to its exercise. . . . There is no undefined residuum of power which he can exercise because it seems to him to be in the public interest.

The Supreme Court has on occasion given support to both of these positions. In several historic cases, it has supported the use of broad executive power to meet emergencies. At the time of the great Pullman railway strike in 1894, for example, President Cleveland sent troops to Chicago to keep the trains running, and had his Attorney General secure a federal court injunction against the strikers. There was no explicit statutory basis for the injunction, but the Court sustained it on the ground that the right of self-preservation must belong to a government, whether claimed by statute or not, and that the executive was constitutionally entitled to act in such cases.

On the other hand, the Supreme Court in the 1952 steel seizure case, *Youngstown Sheet & Tube Co. v. Sawyer,* rebuked the action of President Truman in taking over the steel mills to prevent a strike that would have interrupted the production of munitions for American troops in Korea. There was no law of Congress authorizing this seizure. More important, Congress had in 1947 actually considered giving the President seizure power for such emergencies and had decided against it. Instead, Congress adopted the Taft-Hartley provision authorizing the President to get a court injunction imposing an 80-day "cooling off" period when such strikes were threatened. The Court majority thought that in these circumstances the President was obligated to use the remedy Congress had provided, though Chief Justice Fred M. Vinson and two other dissenting justices charged that the Court was imposing a "messenger boy" concept on the President.

This judicial denial of presidential power was a precedent for the most dramatic conflict between the executive and the judiciary in American history, the Watergate case of *United States v. Nixon* (1974), where the Court rejected Nixon's claim that his decisions on executive privilege were not subject to judicial review. This case will be placed in context later in this chapter.

APPOINTMENT AND REMOVAL

The appointment power (Article II, section 2) is the President's most powerful instrument for effectuating control of the executive branch and significantly influencing the judiciary. The principal limitations on this power derive from the necessity of securing Senate confirmation for appointment to a very large number of offices, a number extending far beyond positions with substantial policy-forming powers. On the other hand, the President's appointments to his White House staff are not subject to confirmation.

The occasional Senate rejection of a presidential nominee takes place under two circumstances. First, nominees who are to fill federal field positions in a state (including judges in the lower federal courts) may be rejected because a senator for that state refuses to agree to the selection, in which event the rule of senatorial courtesy usually results in rejection of the nomination. Second, a majority of the Senate may refuse to confirm a nominee because he is deemed unqualified for the post or, for some other reason, personally unfit or politically undesirable. Examples are the rejections of Nixon nominees Clement F. Haynsworth and G. Harold Carswell for the Supreme Court, and Eisenhower nominee Lewis B. Strauss as Secretary of Commerce. Such rejections are embarrassing defeats for the President, but they occur very rarely.

As for removal, impeachment is the only method mentioned in the Constitution. There is no language pertaining to the President's power to remove or declaring whether officers appointed with confirmation of the Senate can be removed by the President without Senate approval. However, the President's sole control of the removal power was practically unquestioned until after the Civil War. Then, in the bitter feud between Congress and President Andrew Johnson, Congress sought to capture a share in the removal power. The Tenure of Office Act passed in 1867 denied the President's right to remove the heads of executive departments without the advice and consent of the Senate. A violation of this act, which Johnson contended was unconstitutional, was one of the charges on which he was impeached. The act was repealed in 1887 without any Supreme Court ruling on its validity.

In 1876, Congress passed an act providing for Senate participation in the removal of postmasters. Litigation under this statute finally resulted in a long-delayed vindication of Johnson's position in the case of *Myers v. United States* (1926). Myers, a postmaster in Portland, Oregon, was removed by President Wilson before the expiration of his four-year term without securing Senate consent. Myers sued for his salary for the remainder of his term, but the Supreme Court denied his claim on the ground that the 1876 act was unconstitutional.

Chief Justice William Howard Taft, who knew what the presidency looked like from the inside and how important the removal power was, wrote the Court's opinion. He relied upon historical practice and also on the constitutional provisions vesting "executive power" in the President and charging him with faithful execution of the laws.

Though this decision could apply only to the type of position actually involved, Taft asserted that the principle of sole presidential responsibility would apply to all officers, even those to whom Congress had given "duties of a quasi judicial character . . . and members of executive tribunals." Nine years later the Supreme Court had to pass on a case of precisely this character when a member of the Federal Trade Commission was removed by President Franklin D. Roosevelt without any showing of cause, although the statute specified "inefficiency, neglect of duty, or malfeasance in office" as grounds for presidential removal. In *Humphrey's Executor v. United States* (1935) the Court unanimously held this language to be a valid restriction on the removal power.

Justice George Sutherland, writing the Court's opinion, pointed out that the office involved in the *Myers* case, a postmaster, was "restricted to the performance of executive functions," and rather lowly ones at that. In contrast, Humphrey was a member of "an administrative body created by Congress to carry into effect legislative policies embodied in the statute," performing its duties "without executive leave." The Federal Trade Commission is a quasi-legislative" or "quasi-judicial" agency, which Congress intended to discharge its duties "independently of executive control." Forbidding the President to remove its commissioners except for cause is a legitimate way of implementing that policy, "for it is quite evident that one who holds his office only during the pleasure of another, cannot be depended upon to maintain an attitude of independence against the latter's will."

It was rather generally thought from the *Humphrey* decision that the Court would require Congress actually to express by legislation its intention to limit the President's removal power before such limitation would be judicially recognized. However, in *Wiener v. United States* (1958), the Court extended the *Humphrey* principle to cover a quasi-judicial officer where there had been no specific statutory language protecting against removal. Under the *Wiener* decision, then, the President's power of removal, which normally can be exercised at his discretion, may be used against quasi-judicial officers only for cause.

FOREIGN RELATIONS

The provisions of the Constitution pertaining to foreign relations take the form of assignments of particular functions to the various branches of the government. They do not by any means cover the whole range of foreign affairs, and there is no grant of authority over foreign relations in broad terms comparable with the authorization to regulate commerce among the states and with foreign nations. However, such a grant is not necessary. Authority over foreign affairs is an inherent power, which attaches automatically to the federal government as a sovereign entity, and derives from the Constitution only as the Constitution is the creator of that sovereign entity.

The principal theoretical writers on whom the founders relied—Blackstone, Locke, Montesquieu—were unanimous in contending that the power to carry on foreign relations must be vested in the executive. Nevertheless, the Constitution allocated the power to declare war to Congress. It made the Senate's consent necessary to the ratification of treaties and by a two-thirds vote. It made the Senate's advice and consent a condition to the appointment of ambassadors. When account is taken of the general lawmaking and appropriating powers of Congress, the exercise of which is often essential to the formulation and execution of foreign policy decisions, it is clear that "the Constitution, considered only for its affirmative grants of powers capable of affecting the issues, is an invitation to struggle for the privilege of directing American foreign policy."[1]

For this struggle the President is powerfully equipped by the general characteristics of executive power already noted, by his constitutional authority as Commander in Chief, and by his recognized position as "the Nation's organ for foreign affairs," to quote a phrase first used by John Marshall. The powers that the President exercises as "sole organ" can be briefly indicated.

He is the channel for communications to and from other nations and conducts negotiations directly or through his appointed representatives. He has the power of recognizing foreign governments. He can use his control of the armed forces to implement his policies and to protect American rights or interests abroad. To a considerable degree, these powers cancel out the most important grant of external authority to Congress, the power to declare war. For the President can, by his management of foreign affairs and his use of the armed forces, so shape the nation's policy and the development of events as to leave Congress no choice but to declare war. In fact, as the experience in Vietnam showed, the President can commit several hundred thousand American troops in a large-scale military operation without any declaration of war at all.

On the other hand, the necessity of securing Senate consent by a two-thirds vote for the ratification of treaties has proved in practice to be a real limitation on executive policy making—for example, preventing the entrance of the United States into the League of Nations after World War I. Partly because of the hazards of Senate treaty approval, the President has made extensive use of "executive agreements" with foreign countries; these do not require Senate assent. They may be employed for minor matters which it would be inappropriate to embody in a treaty, but often they deal with matters of major importance. Unless such agreements are based on acts of Congress authorizing them, they are usually said to find their constitutional authority in the President's power as Commander in Chief or in his position as the sole organ of international relations. Efforts to distinguish between the legal effects of treaties and executive agreements have generally been unsuccessful.

Article VI sets up treaties and acts of Congress on a par—both are "the supreme law of the land." In case of conflict between a treaty and a statute, the later in point of time generally supersedes the earlier.

---

[1] Edward S. Corwin, *The President: Office and Powers,* New York University Press, New York, 1957, p. 171.

According to Article VI, laws must be made "in pursuance" of the Constitution in order to have status as supreme law of the land, but treaties need only be made "under the authority of the United States." Considerable effort has been made to conjure up from this difference in wording the bogey of a treaty power unlimited by the Constitution. Some substance may seem to be given these fears by the fact that the Supreme Court has never held a treaty unconstitutional, and by the circumstances of the Court's decision in *Missouri v. Holland* (1920). There the Court held that a treaty entered into with Canada for the control of the shooting of wild game gave Congress power to adopt a regulatory statute in this area that it would have had no authority to pass in the absence of the treaty.

Admittedly, this was a somewhat startling holding, but it was the inevitable consequence of the plenary nature of federal power over foreign affairs. The complete incapacity of the states for foreign relationships requires that the federal government have authority to deal with all matters that are of legitimate concern to American foreign relations. This does not mean, however, that the treaty power can be used to amend the Constitution, nor does it open up constitutional rights to revision by treaties.

During the 1950s, American isolationists sought to raise doubt on these points as part of the campaign to secure adoption of the Bricker amendment. The first section of the amendment, in its 1953 version, read: "A provision of a treaty which conflicts with this Constitution shall not be of any force or effect." However, this was clearly already the law on the subject. Any doubt on this score was removed in 1957 when the Court specifically held in *Reid v. Covert* that Article VI did not permit the United States "to exercise power under an international agreement without observing constitutional prohibitions."

COMMANDER IN CHIEF

The President's tremendous executive authority is even further expanded by his status as Commander in Chief. In No. 69 of *The Federalist,* Hamilton thought that the President's role as Commander in Chief would amount "to nothing more than the supreme command and direction of the military and naval forces, as first general and admiral of the Confederacy," while the more significant powers of declaring war and raising and regulating fleets and armies would be exercised by Congress. Actually, this was an accurate enough forecast of the limited role of the Commander in Chief from 1789 to 1861. It was President Lincoln who, in his resolve to save the Union, linked together with the presidential power to take care that the laws be faithfully executed with that of Commander in Chief to yield a result approaching constitutional dictatorship.

For 10 weeks after the fall of Fort Sumter until he called Congress into special session, Lincoln met the emergency by a series of actions that were for the most part without statutory authorization, though they were subsequently ratified by Congress. He added 40,000 men to the Army and Navy, closed the Post Office to treasonable correspondence, paid out 2 million dollars from unappropriated funds in the Treasury, proclaimed a blockade of Southern ports, suspended the writ of habeas corpus in several areas, and caused the arrest and military detention of persons suspected of treasonable practices. World Wars I and II, with their progressively greater impact on the civilian economy of the country, saw a proportionate increase in the President's wartime powers, though the expansion was achieved in nearly all cases with greater regard for the constitutional proprieties than was characteristic of the Civil War.

Lincoln's suspension of the writ of habeas corpus led to one of the great decisions in this field, *Ex parte Milligan* (1866). In a proclamation of September, 1862, Lincoln suspended the writ and ordered that all persons "guilty of any disloyal practice affording aid and comfort to the rebels" should be liable to trial by military commissions. Milligan was arrested at his home in Indiana late in 1864, tried by a military commission, and sentenced to be hanged. In May, 1865, he secured a writ of habeas corpus from the federal court in Indianapolis, and a year later the Supreme Court ruled unanimously that the President had no power to order trial of civilians by military courts in areas where the regular courts were open and operating.

There was a considerable similarity between Lincoln's military commissions and the situation that prevailed in Hawaii during the greater part of World War II. Martial law was declared by the Governor of Hawaii immediately after the Japanese attack on December 7, 1941, and the President approved his action two days later. Civil and criminal courts were forbidden to try cases, and military tribunals replaced them during most of the duration of the war. In 1946, well after the end of hostilities, the Supreme Court held in *Duncan v. Kahanamoku* that when Congress in the Hawaii Organic Act had granted the governor power to declare martial law it had not meant to supersede constitutional guarantees of a fair trial by civil courts that apply elsewhere in the United States.

One of the most shameful wartime actions was the compulsory evacuation of persons of Japanese descent, most of whom were American citizens, from the West Coast after the beginning of World War II. The evacuation, proposed by the military and ordered by the President in February, 1942, was shortly thereafter ratified by Congress, and the Supreme Court had to consider whether it would oppose the joint judgment of the President and Congress that this harsh action was required by military necessity. In *Korematsu v. United States* (1944), the constitutionality of the evacuation program was upheld on the ground that the military authorities were not unjustified in concluding that the Japanese residents of the Coast area constituted a potentially grave danger to the public safety, a danger so great and pressing that there was no time to set up procedures for determining the loyalty or disloyalty of individual Japanese.

CONGRESS VERSUS THE COMMANDER IN CHIEF

Participation in the control of the use of military power, which the Constitution seemed to guarantee to Congress by granting it the power to declare war, has been progressively reduced. In the present century, both Roosevelts, Wilson, Truman, Eisenhower, Kennedy, Johnson, and Nixon have all moved American troops into action or across national frontiers with little or no effort to secure advance congresssional assent. Since 1950, there have been presidential moves into Korea, Lebanon, Cuba, the Dominican Republic, Vietnam, Cambodia, and Laos, as well as distant naval operations, undercover plots, military advisory programs, and aerial overflights of foreign countries that risked conflict, with no opportunity for congressional review.

The disastrous involvement in Indochina was accomplished by the use of Commander-in-Chief powers by four different presidents. After the initial commitment of American advisers and a small number of troops in Vietnam by Presidents Eisenhower and Kennedy, President Johnson used the occasion of an alleged (and probably nonexistent) North Vietnamese torpedo-boat attack on two United States destroyers in the Gulf of Tonkin to ask Congress for a joint resolution of support to strengthen his hand. Almost unanimously, Congress adopted the Tonkin Gulf Resolution approving and supporting "the determination of the President, as Commander in Chief, to take all necessary measures to repeal any armed attack against the forces of the United States and to prevent further aggression."

President Johnson subsequently relied on this resolution as authorizing and justifying the tremendous escalation of military operations in Vietnam and the bombing of North Vietnam, whereas many congressmen felt there had been no such intention and that they had been manipulated into a position where they had to approve the resolution or given an impression of national disunity.

Efforts by members and committees of Congress to recapture some control of the war-making power were tremendously accelerated in 1970 by President Nixon's precipitate expansion of American military activities into Cambodia without any prior consultation with Congress, but they had only limited success. The Cooper-Church amendment of 1970 banned the use of funds for American ground combat forces in Laos, Thailand, and Cambodia. Later that year Congress repealed the Tonkin Gulf Resolution, but this had no effect since by then the official justification for continued military operations was the necessity to protect American troops until they could be withdrawn from Vietnam. Various "end the war" and withdrawal resolutions failed, but Congresss did order the bombing of Cambodia stopped by August 15, 1973.

A number of suits against the war were brought in the courts, usually charging that the war was unconstitutional since it had not been declared by Congress. However, the Supreme Court rejected all efforts to be drawn into what it regarded as a controversy which the political branches would have to settle.

Ultimately congressional frustration over its own impotence did produce an important new statute, the War Powers Act, passed in 1973 over President Nixon's veto. The law sets a 60-day limit on any presidential commitment of United States troops abroad without specific congressional authorization. The commitment can be extended for another 30 days if necessary for the safe withdrawal of troops. Unauthorized commitments can be terminated prior to the 60-day deadline through congressional adoption of a concurrent resolution, a measure which does not require presidential signature. While President Nixon condemned the War Powers Act as an unconstitutional and dangerous restriction on the power of the Commander in Chief to meet emergencies, some members of Congress voted against it on the opposite ground that the statute in fact recognized the President's right to start a war.

Clearly, Congress is at a severe disadvantage in competing with the President for control of foreign policy. In an age when nuclear-armed intercontinental missiles can come hurtling at American cities with only a few minutes' warning, congressional declarations of war seem hopelessly old-fashioned. The Vietnam experience demonstrates the need of finding some more feasible method for reconciling executive power with legislative control. The effectiveness of the War Powers Act for this purpose remains to be determined.

THE PRESIDENCY UNDER RICHARD NIXON

The Presidency of Richard Nixon brought to a head some long-standing concerns about the awesome power and lack of responsibility of the office. In the area of foreign relations, to be sure, Nixon largely followed patterns established by Truman in Korea, Kennedy in Cuba, and Johnson in Vietnam and the Dominican Republic. But, while Nixon did end the Vietnam war which his predecessors had begun, he continued it for four years, long after public support had been withdrawn, and at a cost of 20,000 additional American lives lost, secret bombings of Cambodia, extension of the ground war, and the final Christmas bombing of North Vietnam.

It was in the domestic field, however, that Nixon's exploitation of the powers of the office led to charges of an "imperial Presidency." Here also, of course, there were precedents to follow. Since Franklin Roosevelt, the executive office had burgeoned at the expense of Congress, and it had become accepted doctrine that a powerful President was required to deal with national problems. But Nixon went beyond previous Presidents in several major respects.

One was the degree to which he centralized executive power in the White House by greatly increasing the size of the White House staff, the key members of which took over, from the departments, major policy-forming functions. The transfer of foreign policy from the State Department to Henry Kissinger's White House office was only the most striking instance of this shift. Nixon's ultimate plan, which was aborted by Watergate, was to make all the government's domestic operations responsible to four supersecretaries with offices in the White House.

A second factor was Nixon's attitude of distrust and near-contempt for Congress. Isolated in the White House, with access to the Oval Office controlled by arrogant assistants lacking in political experience and with his introverted personality which prevented him from being at ease or dealing directly with friends or opponents, Nixon made little effort to develop congressional contacts or win congressional cooperation. Congress was to be ignored, threatened, or overridden. Of course Nixon's assumption about congressional ineptitude and weakness was largely justified. But under his attacks Congress did begin to understand the necessity for its own rehabilitation, as evidenced by passage of the War Powers Act and the Budget Reform Act.

It was the Watergate scandals, however, which provoked an unprecedented reexamination of the constitutional position of the Presidency. Separation of powers problems that previously had been only subjects for speculation by constitutional scholars suddenly erupted in newspaper headlines and TV commentaries. The major issue was the validity of the claim of "executive privilege," which Nixon raised to justify denying White House tapes and other records demanded by the congressional investigating committees, the Watergate Special Prosecutor, and judges in several Watergate prosecutions. Nixon's position was that executive privilege had been asserted by all Presidents going back to Washington, that his discussions with members of the White House staff were protected by the necessity of confidentiality, and that the principle of separation of powers guarantees each of the branches of government the right to defend itself against incursions by the other branches.

Prior to Watergate, the Nixon administration had invoked executive privilege principally on foreign relations issues. As the Senate Watergate Committee began operations, Nixon forbade any of his White House aides to testify, a position from which he quickly withdrew under pressure, and in fact the Ervin committee did hear testimony of all relevant White House and Reelection Committee aides.

When the existence of the White House tapes became known, the Senate committee issued subpoenas for some of them, which the White House refused to honor. Court enforcement of the subpoena was subsequently denied by Judge Gerhard Gesell on the ground that making the tapes public might prejudice pending Watergate criminal prosecutions.

When the House Judiciary Committee began its impeachment inquiry, it likewise subpoenaed tapes and was similarly rebuffed. The committee chose not to seek court enforcement, on the ground that such action would be inconsistent with the congressional claim of complete and sole authority on impeachment matters. Instead, the committee took direct action, charging Nixon with contempt of Congress for his refusal in the third article of impeachment.

The Special Watergate Prosecutor was more successful. Archibald Cox's subpoena for tapes and documents to be submitted to the Watergate grand jury was enforced by Judge John J. Sirica, who ruled on August 29, 1973 that the courts had power to pass on the President's claim of executive privilege and to issue a subpoena to the President, as John Marshall had done in the trial of Aaron Burr. Recognizing that there was some need to protect presidential privacy, Sirica indicated that he would himself review the subpoenaed materials to screen out any matter where executive privilege was validly invoked, and then pass the rest on to the grand jury. Sirica's ruling was upheld by the court of appeals, and Nixon then compiled without appealing to the Supreme Court.

The Supreme Court's turn came in 1974. In preparation for the major Watergate coverup trial of Mitchell, Haldeman, Erlichman, and three others, Special Prosecutor Leon Jaworski, appointed to replace Cox after the "Saturday night massacre," subpoenaed some sixty-four tapes. Judge Sirica ordered compliance, and the Supreme Court agreed to a direct review of his decision, bypassing the court of appeals. In *United States v. Nixon,* decided July 24, 1974, the Court unanimously denied the President's right to make a final, unreviewable decision on executive privilege.

Neither the doctrine of separation of powers, nor the need for confidentiality of high-level communications, without more, can sustain an absolute, unqualified, presidential privilege of immunity from judicial process under all circumstances.

The Court did agree that there was a limited executive privilege with a constitutional base, mentioning particularly the need to protect military, diplomatic, or sensitive national security secrets, and assured that the courts would recognize claims of confidentiality related to the President's ability to discharge his constitutional powers effectively. But no national security claims were involved here. There was only "the generalized assertion of privilege," which "must be considered in light of our historic commitment to the rule of law," and "must yield to the demonstrated specific need for evidence in a pending criminal trial."

Watergate also raised some questions concerning the personal amenability of the President to the judicial process. It has been generally assumed that the courts have no practical enforcement powers against the President. John Marshall did not attempt to enforce a subpoena against Jefferson. In *Mississippi v. Johnson* the Supreme Court declined to issue an injunction against the President, pointing out that if the President refused obedience, the Court would be "without power to enforce its process." When Judge John Sirica subpoenaed Nixon's tapes for the grand jury's use, he considered it immaterial "that the court has not the physical power to enforce its order to the President." He simply relied on "the good faith of the executive branch." In fact Nixon did yield to all court subpoenas, although prior to the Supreme Court's decision in *United States v. Nixon* his counsel had refused to give assurance that Nixon would obey a Supreme Court order. It was generally agreed that if such resistance had occurred, it would have been cause for immediate impeachment.

A final issue is whether the President is subject to criminal indictment while in office. It has been generally assumed that a sitting President cannot be prosecuted criminally, and that the only recourse against him is impeachment.[2] The Watergate grand jury unanimously concluded on the basis of the evidence they heard that Nixon had participated in the cover-

[2]For the opposing view that a President can be prosecuted while in office, see Raoul Berger, "The President, Congress, and the Courts: Must Impeachment Precede Indictment?" *Yale Law Journal, 83*: 1111, 1123–1136, 1974.

up, but because they were told by Jaworski that the President cannot be indicted, they listed him as an "unindicted coconspirator." The Supreme Court, on request of Nixon's counsel, agreed to decide whether an incumbent President can be named in this manner, but after consideration the justices ruled in *United States v. Nixon* that the issue was irrelevant and so failed to express an opinion on it.

Under the pressure of the opinion Nixon finally revealed to his counsel and staff the evidence of his complicity in the coverup, and after several days of indecision resigned effective August 9, 1974. By so doing he retained pension rights and other perquisites extended by law to ex-Presidents, which he would have forfeited had he been convicted of impeachment. The impeachment proceedings were aborted, the Judiciary Committee simply submitting a final report to the House. The Ford administration subsequently appeared to assume that a President resigning his office to avoid impeachment for high crimes and misdemeanors was nonetheless entitled to the same privileged status as all other ex-Presidents.

THE PARDONING POWER

The Constitution makes it clear that after a President leaves office he can be prosecuted for criminal acts performed in office, even if he has already been convicted on impeachment for those acts (Article I, section 3). Richard Nixon faced various legal challenges following his resignation. A proposal that Congress grant him immunity from criminal prosecution was dropped, and in any event it could have had no binding effect. But on September 9, only one month after taking office, President Ford suddenly and without consultation with any responsible political figures announced a "full, free and absolute pardon unto Richard Nixon for all offenses against the United States which he, Richard Nixon, has committed or may have committed or taken part in during the period from January 20, 1969, through August 9, 1974."

The power to pardon, granted to the President by Article II, section 2, is usually thought of as an act of grace to correct convictions or sentences which seem mistaken, harsh, or disproportionate to the crime. A pardon may also be sought to restore civil rights lost because of a criminal conviction. The Supreme Court said in *Ex parte Garland* (1867): "When the pardon is full, it releases the punishment and blots out of existence the guilt, so that in the eye of the law the offender is as innocent as if he had never committed the offence."

Ford's pardon of Nixon, who had chosen Ford as Vice President, was widely condemned. Leaving aside unfounded charges of a "deal," criticism centered on the abruptness and secrecy of the action, the fear that the pardon would prevent the full Watergate story from being made public, the effect the pardon would have on the pending trial of six Nixon aides, and the granting of the pardon in advance of any criminal charge. On the latter point, it is true that *Ex parte Garland* asserts that pardon for an offense may be granted "at any time after its commission, either before legal proceedings are taken, or during their pendency, or after conviction and judgment." However, this statement was dictum, and does not consider the serious constitutional issue raised by granting a pardon in advance of the filing of charges, thus completely aborting any possible judicial process. Ford's pardon spoke of offenses which Nixon "has committed," but only courts can decide whether crimes have been committed. Ford contended that acceptance of the pardon by Nixon constituted an admission of guilt, but Nixon himself denied any criminal acts.

ELECTION

The original method of selecting the President called for each state to "appoint, in such manner as the legislature thereof may direct, a number of electors, equal to the whole number of Senators and Representatives to which the State may be entitled in the Congress." The electors were to "meet in their respective States, and vote by ballot for two persons, of whom one at least shall not be an inhabitant of the same State with themselves."

The results of the vote were to be transmitted to the President of the Senate, who would open the sealed certificates in the presence of both houses; and the votes would then be counted. The person with the greatest number of votes was to be the President, provided he had a majority of the whole number of electors. If two candidates were tied, and both had more than a majority, the House was immediately to choose between them. If no candidate had a majority, then the House would choose from the five highest on the list. In either event, the House was to vote by states, "the representation from each State having one vote," and a majority was required to elect. After the choice of President, the person having the next greatest number of votes was to be Vice President; and, in the event of a tie, the Senate was to choose between the contenders.

This arrangement proved faulty very quickly. After Washington's two terms, the two newly developed political parties took over the task of choosing the electors, who then ceased to have any will of their own. The 1796 balloting gave the Presidency and Vice Presidency to different parties, John Adams and Thomas Jefferson ranking first and second in the electoral voting. In 1800, a tie resulted because Jefferson and Aaron Burr, the Republican candidates for President and Vice President, were voted for by each Republican elector. Everyone understood that Jefferson was the presidential choice, but the tie threw the election in the House, where it took all Hamilton's efforts to dissuade the lame-duck Federalists from giving the post to Burr.

This experience led to adoption of the Twelfth Amendment in 1804, and it still largely controls the electoral process. It made the following changes: (1) the electors were to ballot separately for President and Vice President; (2) if no candidate for President received a majority, the House, voting as before by states, was to choose "from the persons having the highest numbers not exceeding three on the list"; (3) the Vice President also had to receive a majority of the electoral votes, and if no one achieved a majority, the Senate was to choose between the two highest candidates; and (4) if the choice of President fell to the House, and it had not made a choice by March 4, the Vice President was to act as President.

This system has weathered two great crises, has three times been responsible for electing a President who had fewer popular votes than his leading opponent, and has been the cause of constant criticism. In 1824, there was no majority in the electoral college; and the House chose John Quincy Adams, though Andrew Jackson had a larger electoral and popular vote. In 1876, there was a dispute over 20 electoral votes, and Congress ultimately set up a completely extraconstitutional electoral commission to decide which votes to accept. This body, with an 8 to 7 Republican majority, decided in favor of the Republican electors; and Rutherford B. Hayes, with a popular vote minority, was elected by one electoral vote. In 1888, Benjamin Harrison was the winner in the electoral college, though receiving 100,000 fewer popular votes than Grover Cleveland.

Normally, the electoral vote magnifies the popular vote margin of the winning candidate, largely because each state casts its entire block of electoral votes for the winner in that state. Other factors in distortion of the popular vote by the electoral result are the overweighting of the less populous states in the electoral college, and the varying rate of voter turnout in different states.

Another feature of the present system is that electors may refuse to cast their ballots in accordance with the results of the balloting in their state. In the elections of 1948, 1956, 1960, 1968, and 1972, one elector on each occasion failed to vote for the candidates of the party that he represented. Moreover, in 1960 eight "unpledged" electors from Mississippi and six from Alabama were elected in a throwback to the original electoral plan that challenged the principle of direct election.

Three main proposals for reform of the electoral system have been made. The first, simplest and most democratic, would require the President to be chosen in a direct nationwide popular election. This plan would abolish the electoral college and guarantee that the candidate receiving the most popular votes would be elected President. Equitably, it would terminate the unit vote advantage of the large states and the electoral vote overweighting of the small states.

A second proposal would retain the existing electoral vote distribution but would have electors chosen from the congressional districts. However, the two electors to which each state is entitled by reason of its two senators would continue to be chosen on the basis of the statewide popular vote.

The third proposal would also continue to assign electoral votes as at present (though the electors would be abolished), but the electoral vote of each state would be divided exactly in proportion to the popular vote each candidate received in the state, percentages being carried three places beyond the decimal point.

The sponsors of both the proportional and the district plans make much the same case aginst the present electoral system. They hope to broaden the base for selection of presidential and vice presidential candidates by decreasing the premium on nominees from the pivotal states. They want to reduce the excessive campaign importance of large, doubtful states. They wish to check the political power of large cities and especially of key minority groups within those cities. They desire to limit to some degree the currently excessive potential effects of local frauds, bad weather, intense local issues, and other accidental circumstances on the determination of electoral votes. They hope to increase the likelihood of a stronger two-party system throughout the country.

On the other hand, it should be pointed out that reducing the electoral importance of the large states with their metropolitan centers would automatically enhance the power of the rural areas, which are already over-represented in the Senate. Moreover, under a proportionate plan the one-party states, which are predominantly rural, would have much greater influence. Thus a proportionate plan would merely create new imbalances in place of the old ones.

Adoption of the direct election alternative was long regarded as impossible because it was assumed that the small states would never give up their overweighting in the electoral college. However, both the American Bar Association and the national Chamber of Commerce recommended it in 1966, and polls of the public and state legislatures showed surprisingly strong support for it. In 1968 the presence of a third party candidate, George Wallace, in the presidential race posed the threat that no one would secure a majority in the electoral college and that the election would be thrown into the House with unpredictable results. Consequently there was much interest in a direct election constitutional amendment sponsored by Sen. Birch Bayh which passed the House in 1969 by a vote of 339 to 70. However, it was defeated in the Senate in 1970 when two efforts to stop a filibuster by imposing cloture failed. Opponents of the direct election plan argued that it would require nationally uniform franchise regulations, maximize the impact of election frauds in close elections, encourage splinter parties to enter candidates, and make candidate effectiveness on television the determining factor in electoral success.

More recently, attention has tended to shift from the method of electing the President to the nominating process and the financing of presidential elections. The methods by which the Republican Party raised $60 million for the 1972 campaign, and the corrupting effect of so much money, resulted in adoption of a new federal campaign finance law by Congress as well as stricter statutes in a number of states. At the same time, the fiasco of the 1972 Democratic convention, selected on strictly representative principles, yet nominating an unelectable candidate, revived interest in proposals for a national presidential primary system.

SUCCESSION

The language of Article II, Section 1, on succession to the Presidency was rather obscure, but constitutional practice has now determined its meaning. The provision is: "In case of the removal of the President from office, or of his death, resignation, or inability to discharge the powers and duties of the said office, the same shall devolve on the Vice President." It is not clear from this wording whether it is the "office" of President that devolves on the Vice President or only the "powers and duties" of the office. If the latter is the intention, then the Vice President would become only an acting President. However, John Tyler, the first Vice President to face this problem, asserted his claim to full presidential status after the death of President William Henry Harrison in 1841; and this precedent has been fully accepted.

The Constitution authorizes Congress to declare what "officer shall . . . act as President" in case neither the President nor Vice President is living or able to serve. Congress in 1792 provided that the succession would pass first to the President pro tempore of the Senate and then to the Speaker of the House. It also required immediate steps to be taken for choosing a new President through the electoral college for a regular four-year term.

In 1886, Congress adopted a different theory of presidential succession, providing that the heads of the seven Cabinet departments then existing, beginning with the Secretary of State, should constitute the line of succession after the Vice President. This act repealed the 1792 provision requiring immediate election of a new President.

No use ever had to be made of either statutory plan. In 1947, Congress adopted still another succession act, under which the Speaker of the House was to act as President when a successor was needed, but he had first to resign as Speaker. If there was no Speaker, the President pro tempore of the Senate, on resigning his post, was to act as President. In either case, the acting President would serve for the remainder of the entire four-year term. Cabinet officers followed in the line of succession according to the seniority of their departments.

The 1947 act was subjected to much criticism as a less satisfactory solution than the 1886 act that it replaced. However, in 1967 Congress found a solution for the succession problem without repealing the 1947 act, by adopting the Twenty-fifth Amendment, which provides in section 2 that "whenever there is a vacancy in the office of the Vice President, the President shall nominate a Vice President who shall take the office upon confirmation by a majority vote of both houses of Congress."

The first occasion for use of the Twenty-fifth Amendment came in 1973 when Vice President Spiro Agnew pleaded no contest to charges of income tax evasion and resigned. Nixon then named Gerald Ford, House minority leader, as Vice President, and he took office on December 6, 1973, after confirmation by bipartisan votes of 387 to 35 in the House and 92 to 3 in the Senate. Nixon, himself the subject of an impeachment investigation at the time, was thus able to select his possible successor. This possibility became a reality when Nixon resigned on August 9, 1974. President Ford then selected as his Vice President Nelson Rockefeller, with the astounding result that for over two years the nation would have a President and a Vice President not elected by the people.

This experience led to consideration of alternative methods of filling Vice Presidential vacancies, and there were even serious suggestions that the office be abolished. Vice Presidential nominees have usually been hurriedly selected at party conventions for reasons of political balance rather than competence. The office is an awkward one with no duties except to preside over the Senate, a function which Vice Presidents seldom perform. If the office were abolished, a vacancy in the Presidency could be filled temporarily by the Speaker of the House or the Secretary of State as Acting President while a special election was held.

PRESIDENTIAL INABILITY

The Constitution contemplates the necessity of carrying on the work of the Presidency in event of the incumbent's "inability to discharge the powers and duties" of the office through illness or for any other reason. It seems clear that the Constitution intended to permit the Vice President to act as President temporarily in such emergencies, the actual President resuming his post when the emergency was terminated. However, there was enough fear of constitutional complications from having two Presidents at the same time to prevent any use of this authorization on occasions when it might have been appropriate.

President Eisenhower had three serious illnesses in a little more than two years. Each of these emergencies created a temporary power vacuum, which could have been eased by having the Vice President become acting President for a temporary period. In the absence of any legislation or constitutional consensus on this problem, President Eisenhower in March, 1958, made public an agreement he had reached with Vice President Nixon concerning a possible future inability. This agreement called for the Vice President to serve as "acting President, exercising the powers and duties of the office until the inability had ended." Then the President "would resume the full exercise of the powers and duties of the office." President Kennedy entered into a similar agreement with Vice President Johnson in 1961.

The assassination of President Kennedy in 1963 was a grim reminder that the various succession problems had not been solved and led Congress to adopt the Twenty-fifth Amendment in 1965. Section 3 of the amendment gave constitutional recognition to the Eisenhower-Nixon type of arrangement by providing that the President, if unable to discharge the powers and duties of his office, could transfer them to "the Vice President as Acting President" by filing a written declaration of inability with the President of the Senate and the Speaker of the House. The President could resume his powers and duties by a written declaration to the same two officers.

The most difficult problem that the drafters of the Twenty-fifth Amendment foresaw was the possibility that the President might suffer a mental illness and not recognize his inability. Stripping a President of his office against his will is a grave prospect, yet the need for such action could arise. Section 4 consequently provided a formula that it was hoped would protect all interests in such a crisis. The Vice President and a majority of the Cabinet "or such other body as Congress may by law provide" were authorized to declare the President unable to serve by written notice to the heads of the two houses of Congress, and on the filing of such a declaration the Vice President would become acting President.

The President then could resume his powers by written notice to the two houses that the inability had ceased to exist. However, if the Vice President and a majority of the Cabinet (or other designated body) within four days notified Congress that in their opinion the President had not recovered from his disability. Congress would have to decide the issue. It would assemble within 48 hours and reach a decision within 21 days. If two-thirds of both houses voted that the President was unable to discharge his duties, the Vice President would continue as Acting President. Otherwise, the President would resume his office. Hopefully no occasion will ever arise calling for the use of this machinery, but it is a valuable insurance against emergency.[3]

THE FUTURE OF THE PRESIDENCY

It has been customary to regard the Presidency as one of the great successes of the Constitution. In general the system has placed able men in office, and occasionally—as with Washington, Jefferson, Lincoln, and Franklin Roosevelt—men providentially suited to the nation's problems. In the present century only Harding and Coolidge lacked minimum qualifications for the office, though Hoover's very considerable talents were not such as to equip him for understanding or dealing with an economic depression.

But Johnson's tragic entanglement in Vietnam and Nixon's wallow in Watergate shook some of the former confidence in the rightness of the presidential institution. To have two consecutive Presidents, elected by landslides, forced out of office—one by resignation, the other by decision not to seek reelection—was a shattering experience. Was this dual debacle caused by character flaws in the two men, or did it point to flaws in the constitutional system? Does the Presidency impose too great a burden on one man and too great a risk upon the country of being stuck with an unwise choice? What happened to the institutional checks which the Framers thought they had built into the system to detect and restrain executive glorification, adventurism, or misfeasance?

Congressional failure to live up to the Founders' expectations is clearly a major factor. A fractured, leaderless, and badly organized legislature has proved incompetent not only to review executive performance but even to discharge its own constitutional functions, inevitably creating a power vacuum into which successive Presidents have moved. In the aftermath of Watergate there were encouraging signs of a new resolve in Congress, but many of its problems are endemic in an institution composed of two chambers and 535 individualists.

During the long months when Watergate was draining the credibility and moral authority of the Nixon Presidency, there were many compari-

[3]During the last weeks of Nixon's Presidency, when he faced either impeachment or resignation and the government seemed to be coming to a standstill, there were numerous suggestions that he "take the Twenty-fifth" and step down temporarily, allowing Ford to serve as Acting President until Nixon's status was determined. Obviously the Twenty-fifth Amendment was not intended for this kind of situation.

sons with the parliamentary system which can quickly remove a leader in whom the country has lost confidence. But the United States lacks the kind of party system, to say nothing of the tradition, to make a parliamentary system work. Possibly there may be a few features of parliamentary government that could be adapted to American conditions—for example, a question hour in Congress for cabinet members. Again, there is some doubt that the Framers acted wisely when they rejected the idea of a council for the President, a council which might perform a consultative function for the President which the American cabinet of department heads has seldom provided.

On the whole, however, it seems unrealistic to anticipate or recommend structural changes in the executive branch. Nor is it desirable, even if possible, to reduce the power of the President. The problem is not presidential power. The American system is built on a strong Presidency. Any office that commands the black box that can blow up the world is by definition a repository of ultimate power.

But something can be done to revise attitudes toward the President. It is disturbing that in the last half of the twentieth century the office has taken on aspects of the monarchical character that some of the Framers feared when they created it in the eighteenth century. It is a far cry from Jefferson, who walked to his inauguration and afterward waited his turn for dinner at his boarding house, to the present-day White House with its fleet of planes, bubble-top limousines, Secret Service protection, ubiquitous "Hail to the Chief," and army of media men covering every move. It is probably impossible to restore Truman-like simplicity to the White House, but more naturalness and accessibility could bring the office down to somewhat more human dimensions.

The blending of power with responsibility is the key to an effective and democratic presidency. Executive power is temptingly easy to use. To prevent its abuse it must be balanced by a vigorous Congress and an activist judiciary. No structural changes in the executive are required if the President will accept the limitations of his office in a constitutional system of checks and balances. Under Nixon the White House became an imperious command post, contemptuous of Congress and condescending to the courts. This challenge to the constitutional system was met when the Supreme Court by unanimous vote in *United States v. Nixon,* and the House Judiciary Committee by its impressive impeachment proceedings, accomplished for the first time in history the resignation of a President.

REVIEW QUESTIONS

1 What were the difficulties with the original constitutional provisions for election of the President?

2 What are the main proposals now being discussed for revising the system of electing the President?

3 What have been the problems in establishing succession to the Presidency beyond the Vice President?

4 Why has the Vice President never become Acting President during periods when the President is disabled?

5 How has the Twenty-fifth Amendment operated?

6 Contrast the views of President Theodore Roosevelt and President Taft on presidential powers.

7 What limitations can Congress impose on the President's removal power?

8 What are the powers that the President possesses for the control of American foreign relations?

9 What is the difference between treaties and executive agreements?

10 Why does Congress seem to have lost the power to declare war?

5 THE FEDERAL JUDICIARY

The Supreme Court, one of the most distinguished and influential of the world's judicial tribunals, traces its position at the apex of the American judicial system directly to Article III of the Constitution. The members of the Constitutional Convention were clear that there had to be a top-level federal court, but they were less certain whether federal courts "inferior" to the Supreme Court were needed.

It was argued by some that the state courts could be authorized to try federal cases, subject to review by the federal Supreme Court. Others contended that the Constitution should provide for a full federal court system. The final decision was to hand this problem of federal organization to Congress, and in the Judiciary Act of 1789 the advocates of a complete and separate system of federal courts were successful.

ORGANIZATION

The federal judicial system consists of three levels. There are 93 district courts, at least one in each state, and 400 district judges. Trials are held in the district courts before a single judge, except that when the constitutionality of a federal statute is questioned, and in certain other situations, three judges must sit in trial of a case. At the intermediate level are the courts of appeals for each of the 10 circuits and the District of Columbia, with a total of 97 judges. Each appeal is heard by a panel of three or more judges. Decisions of the courts of appeals may go for review to the Supreme Court.

The federal judicial establishment also includes such specialized tribunals as the Court of Claims, the Customs Court, and the Court of Customs and Patent Appeals, with 21 judges. The Court of Claims hears contract claims against the government; the Customs Court deals with questions arising in the administration of the tariff laws; and the Court of Customs and Patent Appeals reviews decisions of the Customs Court and the Patent Office.

On the edge of the judicial system are the so-called "legislative" courts. These are courts established by Congress under some constitutional authority other than Article III. Examples are the former territorial courts of Alaska and Hawaii and the courts of such insular possessions as Guam and the Virgin Islands. These tribunals were created under Article IV, section 3, which gives Congress power to make all needful rules and regulations respecting the territory or other property belonging to the United States. The judge of a "legislative" court can be appointed for a term of years rather than "during good behavior"; his salary is not guaranteed against reduction; and duties not strictly judicial can be required of him and his court. He might also be subject to removal by the President for cause.

The courts of the District of Columbia are created under Article I, section 8, clause 17, giving Congress the power "to exercise exclusive legislation" over the District. These courts have been held to be both "legislative" and "constitutional"; thus the tenure and pay of their judges are protected by Article III, but Congress can authorize them to exercise nonjudicial powers.

JURISDICTION

The jurisdiction of the federal courts is defined by Article III on two different bases—subject matter and nature of the parties involved. The subject matter classifications are (1) all cases in law and equity arising under the Constitution; (2) all cases in law and equity arising under the laws of the United States; (3) all cases in law and equity arising under treaties made under the authority of the United States; and (4) all cases of admiralty and maritime jurisdiction. Any case falling in these four fields can be brought in the federal courts, regardless of who the parties to the controversy may be.

Issues arising under the first three of these headings are referred to generally as "federal questions." Such a case arises whenever an interpretation or application of the Constitution or a federal statute or treaty is essential to a judicial decision. A plaintiff seeking to bring a case in the federal courts on one of these grounds must set forth on the face of his complaint a substantial claim as to the federal question involved. Cases appealed from state supreme courts are often refused review by the Supreme Court on the ground that no substantial federal question is present.

The second basis for federal court jurisdiction is in terms of the parties involved. Article III extends federal jurisdiction to controversies (1) to which the United States is a party; (2) between two or more states; (3) between a state and citizens of another state; (4) between citizens of different states; (5) between a state, or the citizens thereof, and foreign states, citizens, or subjects; and (6) to all cases affecting ambassadors, other public ministers, and consuls. Matters involving these classes of parties can be brought in the federal courts, no matter what the subject matter.

Of these classes, the first and the fourth are by far the most important in the generation of litigation. The United States enters federal courts as a party plaintiff in a great number of civil and criminal suits every year, and it can also be haled into court as a defendant in situations in which it has waived its sovereign immunity and given its consent to be sued. When no consent to sue the government has been given, it may be possible to sue officials acting for the government, particularly if they are alleged to be acting beyond their statutory authority or under an unconstitutional statute.

Suits between citizens of different states are commonly referred to as "diversity of citizenship" cases. The purpose of opening the federal courts to these cases was originally to provide a neutral forum for the determination of such disputes, since the state courts might be biased in favor of their own citizens and against "strangers" from other states. Today there is less likelihood of such bias, and many persons have urged the abolition of this class of federal jurisdiction. In 1958, Congress undertook to reduce the number of such cases in the federal courts by limiting them to disputes involving more than $10,000.

The provision extending federal jurisdiction to suits between a state and citizens of another state was the source of a controversy which resulted in adoption of the Eleventh Amendment. In *Chisholm v. Georgia* (1973) the Supreme Court ruled that this language, which had been generally understood to be an authorization to each state to sue citizens of other states, also permitted citizens to sue a state other than their own. This judicial misreading of constitutional intent aroused a storm in the states, and Congress promptly responded by initiating the Eleventh Amendment to reverse this ruling.

Suits falling under federal jurisdiction can also be brought in state courts, except in those areas—such as federal criminal, admiralty, patent, and bankruptcy cases—in which Congress has given the federal courts exclusive jurisdiction. In all other areas, the state and federal courts enjoy concurrent jurisdiction over Article III cases. A suit meeting the tests of federal jurisdiction that is filed in a state court can by appropriate action be transferred to a federal court for trial. The right of removal of state prosecutions to federal courts is particularly important in civil rights cases in those states where the local courts could not be relied on to give a fair trial to defendants.[1]

Where state courts do exercise federal jurisdiction, they are of course bound by the "supremacy clause" of the Constitution. Article VI, after making the Constitution, laws, and treaties of the United States "the supreme law of the land," continues: "And the judges in every state shall be bound thereby, anything in the Constitution or laws of any state to the contrary notwithstanding."

The complication of a dual system of courts is one which other leading federal governments, such as Australia, Canada, and India, have avoided. In these countries there is only one federal court, superimposed on a complete system of state courts. By contrast, the American system may often seem to be cumbersome and productive of confusion and delays. However, processes of cooperation and adjustment have largely solved the many potential conflicts in our dual system of courts.

---

[1] For illustrative cases, see *Dombrowski v. Pfister* (1965), and *Younger v. Harris* (1971).

JUDICIAL POWER

The judicial power that the Constitution gives the federal courts is the power to determine "cases" and "controversies" of the types specified in Article III. What is a case or controversy? Not every argument or dispute presented in the form of a lawsuit will qualify. To have a case or controversy in the constitutional sense there must be (1) adverse parties (2) who have a substantial legal interest (3) in a dispute arising out of facts, real, not hypothetical, (4) in which there can be an enforceable determination of the rights of the parties. These conditions are so well understood that they customarily raise no difficulties, but they do relieve the Court of passing on some broad public issues that cannot be fitted into the context of a traditional lawsuit.

The courts decide controversies by determining the facts in the dispute and applying the law to those facts. According to the tradition of the English common law, on which American jurisprudence is largely based, the law is a body of general principles of right and justice embodied in the past decisions of the courts. The courts do not make law, it is said; they merely declare what it is in specific cases, applying established principles to new situations as they arise.

That this is, in part at least, a kind of lawmaking becomes obvious in a case in which the precedents are inconclusive or conflicting, or in which there simply are no precedents. Often enough in such a case, a judge lays down a rule based primarily on his own notions of public policy and the general interest and not on any specifically legal or juridical considerations.

The power of the federal courts to enforce their decisions is normally taken for granted, but in fact the courts have no enforcement machinery at their direct disposal except for a few marshals. The judiciary must look to the President and to Congress for help in case of any real resistance to its orders. Andrew Jackson's purported comment, "John Marshall has made his decision, now let him enforce it," reveals the need of the Supreme Court for support by its governmental colleagues and the backing of public opinion.

THE FEDERAL JUDICIARY

The appointment of federal judges is frankly and entirely a political process. With few exceptions, the President limits his choice to members of his own party. From 1933 to 1974, there were only two exceptions to this practice in Supreme Court appointments—President Truman's appointment of Republican Harold Burton, with whom he had been associated in the Senate, and President Eisenhower's naming of Democrat William Brennan, Jr. In the lower federal courts, during the present century more than 90 percent of all judicial appointments have gone to members of the President's party.

District judgeships are filled primarily on the recommendation of the state party organization and the senator from the state, if there is one of the President's party. The "President's men" in the Department of Justice may also originate names and support candidates. The nominees thus suggested are checked by the FBI and the American Bar Association's committee on the federal judiciary. Vacancies on the courts of appeals are sometimes filled by promotion of a district judge; the party organizations are still important in the choices at this level.

For the Supreme Court, the President receives suggestions from many sources, and particularly from his Attorney General, but he makes his own decision, and often he has his own ideas on the subject, either as to specific persons, or as to the qualifications he wants. President Nixon had an unusual set of requirements. His nominees had to be not only Republicans less than 62 years of age but also "strict constructionists" of the Constitution and sitting federal judges. He applied these criteria even to the Chief Justiceship. In contrast to former Presidents, who have generally appointed outstanding public figures like Charles Evan Hughes or Earl Warren as Chief Justice, Nixon named Warren Earl Burger, a little-known federal appellate judge. For the next vacancy, Nixon added still another qualification—the appointee must be from the South. However, his two southern nominees—Clement F. Haynsworth, Jr., and G. Harrold Carswell—were rejected by the Senate as not meeting Supreme Court standards. After bitterly charging the Senate with prejudice against the South, Nixon then named Harry A. Blackmun, a Minnesota federal appellate judge, whom the Senate confirmed unanimously. Only one previous nominee to the Court—John J. Parker—had been rejected in the present century.[2]

For the two vacancies created in 1971 by the retirement and death of Justices Hugo Black and John M. Harlan, Nixon's search for "strict constructionists" led him to propose to the American Bar Association committee for review a slate of six persons, all unknown nationally or clearly unqualified for the high court. The two candidates he preferred were in fact rated as unqualified by the American Bar Association. In a quick switch, Nixon avoided another battle with the Senate by naming two much more able conservatives, Lewis F. Powell, Jr., and William H. Rehnquist.

Appointment of federal judges for "good behavior" is one of the great pillars of judicial independence. A federal judge can be removed from office only by conviction on impeachment. Only one Supreme Court justice has ever been subjected to impeachment proceedings, Samuel Chase, whose judicial conduct was marked by gross and violent Federalist partisanship. In 1804, the triumphant Jeffersonians sought reprisal by way of impeachment, but failed to secure a conviction. Only nine lower federal court judges have been impeached in the entire history of the federal bench; four of them were convicted.

While federal judges can be removed only by impeachment, they can

[2]In 1968 President Johnson's nomination of Justice Abe Fortas as Chief Justice had to be withdrawn when opponents resorted to a filibuster.

be indicted for criminal behavior, and conviction would of course require resignation. Four judges have been indicted, and two convicted. Judge Otto Kerner, appealing his conviction for criminal conspiracy in 1974, argued that he could not be tried until after he had been removed by impeachment, but the Supreme Court refused to hear his case, thereby confirming his conviction. He then resigned.

In 1969 Justice Fortas became the first justice in Supreme Court history to resign because of charges of unethical conduct; he had accepted a retainer for consulting services from a foundation. Heightened concern about judicial ethics played a part in the defeat of the Haynsworth and Carswell nominations. In 1970 conservative members of the House launched an unsuccessful impeachment drive against Justice William O. Douglas, the Court's most liberal member, who had achieved notoriety by his off-the-bench activities, speeches, and publications. Gerald Ford, leading the drive as House minority leader, contended that under the "good behavior" standard the House could impeach a justice for any conduct of which it disapproved.

THE SUPREME COURT AND ITS OPERATION

The Supreme Court was originally composed of six judges, but the number was subsequently both reduced and increased by Congress, usually with political motives in mind. Since 1869, the size has been stable at nine members, and the effort of President Roosevelt to increase the number of justices in 1937 failed. The Court is headed by the Chief Justice of the United States. His formal authority consists primarily in his role as presiding officer in court and at the conferences and in his power to assign the writing of opinions.

There are some special problems of jurisdiction relating to the Supreme Court. It is primarily an appellate court; but the Constitution does define two categories of cases that can be heard in the Court's original jurisdiction, i.e., without prior consideration by any other court. These are cases in which a state is a party, and those affecting ambassadors, public ministers, and consuls. However, the Court generally does not have to accept a suit invoking its original jurisdiction unless it feels that there is a compelling reason of public policy.

All the remaining business of the Supreme Court comes to it in its appellate jurisdiction, which it exercises, as the Constitution says, "with such exceptions, and under such regulations as the Congress shall make." In the post-Civil War period Congress used this authority over the Court's appellate jurisdiction to withdraw from its consideration a politically embarrassing case in which the Court had already heard argument. The Supreme Court agreed that such action was within congressional power. In 1957, Senator Jenner of Indiana sought reprisal against the Court's decisions in certain national security cases by a bill withdrawing the Court's appellate jurisdiction in five specific kinds of cases, but it failed of enactment.[3]

Most of the cases the Supreme Court decides are brought before it by the writ of certiorari. This Latin word, which can be translated as "to be certified," comes from the formal language of the old English writ of certiorari, by which a higher court ordered a lower court to send up the record of a case.

Certiorari is a discretionary writ—that is, the Supreme Court does not have to grant a petition for certiorari and in most instances does not. Petitions are granted only in cases in which at least four of the nine judges agree that issues of special importance are presented.

The role of the Supreme Court is to correct errors of law—that is, mistakes in defining, interpreting, or applying the law—made by the courts below. But not all judicial errors are important enough to require correction by the Supreme Court. In recent years, the Supreme Court has granted less than 10 percent of the petitions for certiorari filed annually.[4] The exercise of the Court's discretion in deciding whether to grant or deny certiorari may involve as much judicial statesmanship as the decision of a case on the merits.

Congress has provided for review by appeal of state court decisions denying a litigant's claim of federal right. A state court is said to have denied a claim of federal right (1) where it upholds a state law that one of the parties contends violates the federal Constitution, or (2) where one of the parties invokes a federal statute or treaty and the state court holds it invalid. Decisions of these types can be appealed from the highest state court "in which a decision could be had."

The Supreme Court meets for business in October of every year, and this "October Term" continues until the following June. The usual pattern of the Court's operation is to hear the arguments of counsel in cases before it for about two weeks at a time and then to recess for two weeks or so to study the cases and write opinions.

On Fridays while the court is sitting, the justices meet in conference to discuss and decide pending cases.[5] At the conference, the Chief Justice presents each case along with his views; and discussion then moves to the associate justices in order of seniority. When the vote is taken, the order is reversed, the most recent appointees to the Court voting first, and

[3]It is generally believed that any legislation seriously curtailing the appellate jurisdiction of the Supreme Court would be declared unconstitutional by the Court, since such a measure would challenge its standing as head of the judicial branch and its authority to make final interpretations of the Constitution. See Raoul Berger, *Congress v. The Supreme Court* Harvard University Press, 1969, chap. 9.

[4]For *in forma pauperis* petitions, the Court grants less than 5 percent. These petitions are without payment of the normal filing fees, and are customarily filed by prisoners challenging the legality of their conviction. Though such petitions are often frivolous, a few have resulted in important rulings, for example, *Gideon v. Wainwright* (1963), which established the right to have counsel assigend in criminal prosecutions.

[5]Beginning with the 1972 term the Court attempted, not always successfully, to reserve Thursdays to prepare for the Friday conference.

the Chief Justice last. Following the vote, the Chief Justice assigns the writing of the Court's opinion to himself or one of his colleagues. If the decision was not unanimous and the Chief Justice voted in the minority, the senior associate justice who voted in the majority controls the assignment of the decision. Drafts of opinions are circulated among the justices, and the author may revise the final opinion on the basis of comments by his colleagues.

In the Court's early days, it was the custom for all justices to give their opinions seriatim in a case; and there was no single opinion "for the Court." However, when John Marshall became Chief Justice in 1801, he decided that the Court's prestige and power would be increased if a single opinion was prepared, and in fact he himself wrote the opinions in almost all important cases. Justices were still free to write concurring or dissenting opinions, but there was a tendency for them to go along with the Court in silence unless their disagreement was sharp. More recent practice permits dissents to be registered much more freely, and nonunanimous decisions now generally outnumber the unanimous ones.

It is a fundamental principle of American and English jurisprudence that a decision by the highest court in a jurisdiction is a binding precedent on the questions of law involved in the case. The court making the decision and all the courts subordinate to it are expected to follow the precedent and to give similar answers to similar questions whenever they arise thereafter. The Latin label for this rule is *stare decisis,* "to stand by the things decided."

Although stare decisis is an ancient and fundamental principle, the Supreme Court does not always follow it. Particularly in constitutional cases, the Court may find it necessary to disregard or overrule its own prior decisions. If the Court will not change its interpretation of the Constitution, it can be accomplished only by a formal amendment. Justice Louis D. Brandeis once wrote:

> Stare decisis is usually the wise policy, because in most matters it is more important that the applicable rule of law be settled than that it be settled right . . . . This is commonly true even where the error is a matter of serious concern, provided correction can be had by legislation. But in cases involving the Federal Constitution, where correction through legislative action is practically impossible, this Court has often overruled its earlier decisions. The Court bows to the lessons of experience and the force of better reasoning, recognizing that the process of trial and error, so fruitful in the physical sciences, is appropriate also in the judicial function.[6]

[6] *Burnet v. Coronado Oil & Gas Co.,* 205 U.S. 393 (1932). In the 1974 case of *Mitchell v. W. T. Grant Co.,* Justice Stewart protested reversal of a principle announced only two years earlier in *Fuentes v. Shevin:* ". . . the Court today has unmistakably overruled a considered decision of the Court that is barely two years old, without pointing to any change in either societal perceptions or basic constitutional understandings that might justify this total disregard of *stare decisis.* . . . The only perceivable change that has occurred is in the makeup of this Court. A basic change in the law upon a ground no firmer than a change in our membership invites the popular misconception that this institution is little different from the two political branches of the Government."

JUDICIAL REVIEW

The most important responsibility of the Supreme Court is to interpret the Constitution of the United States. In carrying out that high duty the Court may find it necessary to nullify state statutes or even acts of Congress as violative of the Constitution.

The basic theory on which the American practice of judicial review is based may be summarized as follows. The written Constitution is a superior law, subject to change only by an extraordinary legislative process involving both Congress and the states, and as such superior to common and statutory law. The powers of the several departments of government are limited by the terms of the Constitution. The judges are expected to enforce the provisions of the Constitution as the higher law and to refuse to give effect to any legislative act or executive order in conflict therewith.

Strangely enough, there is nothing about this in the Constitution itself. The immediate source of the doctrine is the decision of Chief Justice John Marshall in the case of *Marbury v. Madison* (1803). William Marbury had been appointed a justice of the peace for the District of Columbia by President Adams just before he went out of office in 1801. His commission was signed and sealed, but the Federalist Secretary of State, none other than John Marshall, failed to deliver it on March 3, and Jefferson on taking office instructed his Secretary of State, James Madison, not to deliver it. Marbury filed a petition for mandamus to compel Madison to deliver the commission. He filed it in the Supreme Court directly without any prior court proceedings, thus invoking the Court's original jurisdiction under the Judiciary Act of 1789.

A writ of mandamus (Latin for "we command") is an order to a court or a public official to perform some act required by law. The Supreme Court could grant Marbury's petition or deny it. At first glance, it seemed that the Court was bound to lose the contest for power and prestige whichever it did. If the writ was issued, Madison, with Jefferson's support, would refuse to obey it, and the Court would have no practical means of compelling him to do so. If the Court refused relief to Marbury, it would be admitting officially that it lacked any authority to control the executive. In either case, the judiciary and the Federalists would be humiliated and the triumph of Jefferson and the Democrats would be complete and obvious.

Marshall's decision was a masterly stroke. He ruled that the Judiciary Act of 1789, in authorizing the Supreme Court to grant writs of mandamus in its original jurisdiction, had unconstitutionally extended the Court's original jurisdiction beyond that provided for in the Constitution. The Court consequently declined to issue the writ, leaving Madison and Jefferson with nothing to defy or resist. But the writ was refused, not because the Court lacked power to give relief against executive officers, but because the Court asserted and exercised the much greater power of passing on the constitutionality of an act of Congress.

Though the draftsmen of the Constitution had not specifically provided for this power, such evidence as there is of contemporary opinion and practice tends to support Marshall. Furthermore, though Marshall cited no precedent, state courts had already found occasion to strike down state statutes because they were in violation of state constitutions. Alexander Hamilton in No. 78 of *The Federalist* had argued strongly in favor of judicial review, an argument from which Marshall borrowed. And even the Democrats voiced no strong objections to the doctrine at the time, though they denounced Marshall's attempt to instruct Jefferson and Madison in the performance of their official duties. The Chief Justice's arguments may not have been unanswerable, but his conclusion that passing on the constitutionality of acts of Congress is one of the normal functions of the judiciary seems to have been pretty well accepted in 1803. It is, or course, firmly established today.

In more modern times, judicial review has been criticized as undemocratic, in that it turns basic policy decisions over to a lifetime judiciary responsible to no popular will. That there is room for judicial discretion in decisions on constitutionality cannot be doubted. Seldom is a statute so plainly and obviously in violation of the Constitution that there is not room for two opinions about it. Decisions on constitutional issues are likely to be as much a matter of social and economic philosophy as of logical deduction and immutable principles of law, and the fact that these decisions are made by nine men called judges sitting in a marble palace does not change the situation.

One method of countering the undemocratic charge is to admit it and then go on to point out that democratic nature or quality is not the sole test of an institution in the American system. The Constitution does not provide for a simple democratic regime, always directly responsive to majority will, but for a federal representative republic equipped with a number of built-in checks and balances, of which judicial review is one.

Another answer also admits that the Supreme Court is undemocratic, but asserts that it is not dangerously so. The Court, it is said, is inherently so weak that it cannot long defy the settled determination of a substantial majority. When it has tried to do so, it has not been able to maintain its position long. Congress controls some of its jurisdiction, many of its powers, and even the number of its members. The execution of its judgments and the appointment of its members depend on the President. It is consequently by no means immune from popular and political pressures.

Within the present century, there have been three periods in which the Supreme Court's powers of review have become the subject of a major political struggle. One was occasioned by the Court's invalidation of many items in the New Deal's legislative program in 1935 and 1936. President Roosevelt retaliated in 1937 by requesting Congress to authorize 6 additional justices, increasing the Court's size to 15. This effort represented a serious political miscalculation on Roosevelt's part. While it was clear that the country disagreed with the Court's constitutional interpretations, it was equally opposed to any such rude laying of hands on the judicial institution. There are legitimate ways of changing judicial policy, but this was not one of them. Congress defeated the President's proposal, and instead passed a liberalized retirement act to encourage the older justices to leave the bench. Within a short time, resignations permitted President Roosevelt to make over the Court by new appointments, and the judicial threat to executive and legislative policy was ended.

The Supreme Court of the 1950s also encountered a political storm as a result of its decisions on racial segregation in the public schools and certain national security cases in which it upheld the civil rights of Communists or persons accused of being Communists. This time it was Congress rather than the President that mounted an attack on the Supreme Court, but it failed just as completely as the "Court-packing" plan had failed. Again, however, the Court did withdraw from some of the positions that had led to congressional anger, particularly with respect to judicial control over congressional investigating committees.

In the 1960s the Court again aroused opposition by declaring unconstitutional religious observances in the public schools and the apportionment practices of most state legislatures. Constitutional amendments reversing the Court's holdings were introduced in both these areas but were not adopted. However, opposition to certain decisions limiting police tactics in interrogating suspected criminals was more successful. President Nixon in his 1968 campaign charged the Court with contributing to the increase in crime by making convictions more difficult to secure, and a "law and order" majority in Congress specifically challenged several Court decisions in the Crime Control Act of 1968.

JUDICIAL SELF-RESTRAINT

The Supreme Court recognizes, in principle, that its power to construe the Constitution, and particularly its power to declare acts of Congress unconstitutional, must be exercised with great restraint. Consequently it approaches constitutional questions with reluctance, and will normally decide cases on a constitutional issue only when there seem to be no feasible alternatives.

The easiest means of avoiding constitutional questions is, of course, to deny certiorari in cases where such an issue is present, and this the Court sometimes does. Again, in a case which the Court has agreed to hear, decision may be delayed until the heat has gone out of a constitutional question. Several wartime civil liberties cases have not been decided until after the war was over.

The Supreme Court has, furthermore, imposed upon itself a comprehensive body of rule aimed at encouraging judicial self-restraint and avoiding constitutional decisions. As summarized by Justice Brandeis in his concurring opinion in *Ashwander v. Tennessee Valley Authority* (1936), these include the following: (1) The Court will not anticipate a question of constitutionality in advance of the necessity of deciding it, nor is it the habit of the Court to decide questions of a constitutional nature unless absolutely necessary to a decision of the case in hand. (2) The Court will not formulate a rule of constitutional law broader than is required by the precise facts to which it is to be applied. (3) The Court will not pass upon a constitutional question, although properly presented by the record, if there is also present some other ground upon which the case may be disposed of. (4) When the validity of an act of Congress is drawn into question, and even if a serious doubt of constitutionality is raised, it is a cardinal principle that the Court will first ascertain whether a construction of the statute is fairly possible by which the question may be avoided.

Whether or not the Court always follows these rules, they do reflect the general principles of its approach to judicial review. Beyond these maxims of judicial self-restraint, there are certain more technical rules applied to limit the breadth and freedom of the Supreme Court's approach to constitutional issues.

One of these is the rule that the question must be "justiciable." This means that judicial proceedings must meet the tests of cases and controversies already mentioned. The Court will not give "advisory opinions," even if requested by the President, as Washington once did. It is usually quick to detect and to refuse to rule on made-up cases that are in reality nothing but attempts to obtain a Supreme Court ruling on abstract questions of law, or "friendly" lawsuits where the parties on both sides have the same interests.

In 1895, for example, the federal income tax was declared unconstitutional in a suit brought by a corporate stockholder against the corporation to prevent it from paying the tax. It seems unlikely that the corporation fought very hard to uphold its obligation to pay the tax. This particular decision was, in effect, overruled by the adoption of the Sixteenth Amendment; but the problem of representation of the public interest in constitutional litigation was not dealt with until 1937, when Congress provided that the United States must be joined as a party in any case in which the constitutionality of a federal statute was questioned.

An important element of justiciability is "standing to sue." Not everyone with enough money to bring a lawsuit is entitled to litigate the legality or constitutionality of government action in the federal courts. To have the standing necessary to maintain such an action, the plaintiff must establish the sufficiency of his interest in the controversy, and this means satisfying the courts on two main issues: (1) that his interest is one that is peculiar and personal to him and not one he shares with all other citizens generally, and (2) that the interest he is defending is a legally recognized and protected right immediately threatened by some government action. For example, two 1974 cases held that a citizen group had no standing to question the constitutionality of members of Congress holding commissions in the armed forces reserves, and that a taxpayer had no standing to compel the Secretary of the Treasury to make public the budget of the CIA, which is known only to a few key members of Congress.

Lawsuits are customarily brought by, or on behalf of, one or more specifically named individuals. However, where an interest is at stake that is widely shared—for example, access of black children to integrated schools or protection of air or water from pollution—so-called "class suits" may be brought by a few named individuals suing for themselves and "all others similarly situated."

Controversies that meet the test of justiciability are nevertheless occasionally refused adjudication by the Supreme Court on the ground that they involve "political questions." Where the authority to make a certain decision appears to have been assigned by the Constitution exclusively to the Congress or the President, the courts will refuse to interfere, although the case may be otherwise justiciable. The conclusion that the Constitution assigns authority to solve a particular problem to the two political branches of the government is usually supported by practical considerations.

Thus it is generally agreed that the Constitution gives the President almost exclusive authority over American relations with foreign governments. It follows and the courts agree, that a question related to the conduct of foreign affairs is likely to be a political question with which the judiciary should not meddle. Efforts to get the Supreme Court to rule on the contention that the war in Vietnam was unconstitutional because there had been no congressional declaration of war were uniformly unsuccessful. In the case of *United States v. Nixon* the President's counsel argued that a claim of executive privilege was a political action which the courts had no authority to review, but the Supreme Court unanimously rejected this position.

The whole process of amending the Constitution is now regarded by the Supreme Court as a political question within the jurisdiction of Congress. Whether a state has a "republican form of government," such as the Constitution guarantees to every state in Article IV, section 4, is another political question.

In *Colegrove v. Green* (1946), a badly divided Court refused to remedy gross inequalities of population in Illinois congressional districts, where one congressman might represent nine times as many people as a representative from another Illinois district. The Court majority thought it should keep out of this "political thicket." Similarly the Court in 1950 refused to look at the Georgia county unit system for voting in primary elections, though it intentionally discriminated against the large city populations in favor of the rural areas.

In 1962, however, the Supreme Court reversed this position in *Baker v. Carr,* holding that the federal courts could review a claim of malapportionment of seats in the Tennessee state legislature. The Tennessee constitution required reapportionment of the legislature every 10 years, but no action had been taken since 1901, and consequently the districts varied greatly in population. The situation was the same in many of the states, and in general the urban areas were seriously underrepresented in the state legislatures.

After *Baker v. Carr* had opened the courts to complaints about apportionment, an avalanche of suits hit the courts. In *Gray v. Sanders* (1963), the Supreme Court invalidated the Georgia county unit system. Congressional districts, which the Court had refused to consider in the *Colegrove* case, were required by *Wesberry v. Sanders* (1964) to contain substantially equal numbers of people. Then in *Reynolds v. Sims* (1964) the Court declared that the principle of equal protection of the laws required the rule of "one person, one vote" in the states, and that districts roughly equal in population must be the basis for election of representatives to both houses of each state's legislature.

SUMMARY

American courts participate to a significant and unusual degree in the policy-forming process. Appointment of federal judges is political in that they are generally selected by the President from members of his own party and have typically been active politically. However, there are protections in the selection procedure, and the federal bench is of high prestige and unquestioned integrity. Because of their life tenure and independence, the federal judiciary can act as a check on both the President and Congress. The Supreme Court is recognized as the highest authority on the meaning of the Constitution, and it can nullify statutes or executive actions as unconstitutional. The exercise of this power has occasionally led to serious counterattacks on the Court, but in general the power of judicial review has been accepted as one of the valuable safeguards of American democracy.

REVIEW QUESTIONS

1 What are the three levels of the federal judicial system?

2 Why can "diversity of citizenship" cases be tried in federal courts?

3 What are the elements in a judicial "case or controversy?"

4 How are federal judges chosen?

5 How do cases get to the Supreme Court?

6 What is the procedure by which the Supreme Court decides cases?

7 What is the responsibility of the Supreme Court to follow its precedents?

8 What was the dilemma Marshall faced in *Marbury v. Madison,* and how did he solve it?

9 Is judicial review undemocratic?

10 What principles of judicial self-restraint has the Supreme Court announced?

6 INDIVIDUAL RIGHTS

The American tradition of civil rights is composed of many strands. Basic is the Christian-Hebraic belief in the worth of the individual, and acceptance of a moral obligation to shape the institutions of society so that they will promote the unfolding and the enrichment of human character. Centuries of struggle in England to achieve political practices that would aim toward equality before the law and equalization of political power were a living part of the early American tradition. The writings of the seventeenth- and eighteenth-century political philosophers, particularly Locke, with their stress on natural law and the origins of government in a compact freely entered into by its citizens, were an essential element in American revolutionary thought.

All this was the heritage of the new nation, the "common law" of American liberties. If these ideals had never been spelled out in the Constitution, they would no doubt have continued to be effective. But placing them in the Bill of Rights provided a guide for the political decisions of the developing commonwealth and made these principles judicially enforceable.

THE RIGHT TO VOTE

In a very real sense, the right to vote is the foundation on which all other rights are based. The disfranchised can appeal to the sense of justice of the franchise holders, and they can endeavor to protect their rights in the courts, but they can never be full-fledged members of the political community. Without the sanctions of political pressure exercised through the ballot box, their liberties will inevitably be more limited and less secure than those of the voting members of the community. The experience of black Americans in the South over the past century is ample illustration.

The drafters of the Constitution dealt with the franchise problem in a rather indirect manner. They provided in Article 1, section 2, that persons eligible to vote for members of the House in the several states "shall have the qualifications requisite for electors of the most numerous branch of the state legislature." By this method the Constitution[1] assured election of

[1] The drafters of the Constitution had to deal with the franchise problem only in connection with the election of members of the House, since senators were chosen by the state legislatures, and presidential electors were appointed in such manner as the state legislatures might direct.

the House of Representatives on a popular base but avoided creation of a national electorate different from the state electorates, which were defined by legal provisions varying widely from state to state.

Under this arrangement the states determine which of their citizens have the privilege of the franchise. However, once a state has decided by statutory provisions who is eligible to vote, then the Constitution through Article 1, section 2, steps in to guarantee their *right* to vote in federal elections.

In addition, five amendments have a bearing on elections and the electorate. The equal protection clause of the Fourteenth Amendment has been applied to forbid discriminatory practices by state election officials. The Fifteenth Amendment specifically guarantees that "the right of citizens of the United States to vote shall not be denied or abridged by the United States or by any state on account of race, color, or previous condition of servitude." The Nineteenth Amendment, adopted in 1920, uses the same formula to guarantee women the right to vote. The Twenty-fourth Amendment forbids the use of the poll tax as a prerequisite for voting in elections for federal offices. The Twenty-sixth Amendment extends the right to vote to eighteen-year-olds.

Application of constitutional protections to primary elections was for some time in serious question. In 1921, the Supreme Court held that when the Constitution referred to elections, it meant the "final choice of an officer by the duly qualified electors," and that the primary was "in no real sense part of the manner of holding the election." Applying this principle in 1935, the Court ruled that there was no constitutional barrier to exclusion of blacks from the Democratic primaries in Texas, provided the discrimination was not state-authorized and was achieved solely by the action of the political party conducting the primary.

These two notions, that primaries are not part of the election process, and that political parties are in effect "private clubs" that can exclude any persons they do not like from their primaries, were both obviously fallacious, and both were soon abandoned by the Court. The Constitution was held applicable to primaries in *United States v. Classic* (1941), a prosecution brought by the federal government against election officials in Louisiana who had tampered with the ballots in a primary in which candidates for representatives in Congress were chosen. The Court pointed out that the Louisiana election laws made the primary "an integral part" of the process of electing congressmen, and that in fact the Democratic primary in Louisiana was "the only stage of the election procedure" where the voters' choice was of significance.

The private club theory was abandoned in *Smith v. Allwright* (1944). The Court held that after the *Classic* ruling, party primaries could no longer be regarded as private affairs nor the parties conducting them as unaffected with public responsibilities. Noting that parties and party primaries in Texas were in fact regulated at many points by state statutes, the Court reasoned that a party required to follow these directions was "an agency of the State"; and, if it practiced discrimination against blacks, that was "state action within the meaning of the Fifteenth Amendment."

Supreme Court decisions alone, however, were not enough to break up the widespread practice of racial discrimination at the polls, which was accomplished in part by intimidation and violence and in part by barriers imposed by tests for literacy and "understanding" the Constitution. In the Voting Rights Act of 1965 Congress took direct action against the abuse of such tests by suspending the use of literacy tests or similar voter qualification devices in states and voting districts that had less than 50 percent of voting age residents registered in 1964 or actually voting in the 1964 presidential election, and authorized the appointment of federal voting examiners who would go into these areas and register blacks. This act, upheld by the Supreme Court in *South Carolina v. Katzenbach* (1966), had an immediate impact in adding thousands of blacks to the voting rolls and making it possible for black candidates to be elected to public office in the South.

The poll tax, which was an additional bar to voting by blacks and which in 1965 was still a requisite for voting in five states, was also a congressional target. In 1964, the Twentieth-fourth Amendment was adopted barring the poll tax in federal elections. Then, in *Harper v. Virginia State Board of Elections* (1966), the Supreme Court held that the requirement to pay a fee as a condition of obtaining the ballot was an invidious discrimination contrary to the equal protection clause, thus rendering poll tax systems unconstitutional in state elections as well.

When the Voting Rights Act expired in 1970, it was renewed by Congress, but with important additions. Literacy tests were suspended in all states for five years, all citizens who had lived in a state for 30 days were authorized to vote in presidential elections, and the voting age was lowered from twenty-one to eighteen for all federal, state, and local elections. By a 5 to 4 vote the Supreme Court in *Oregon v. Mitchell* (1970) upheld the extension of the franchise to eighteen-year-olds in national elections, but declared it unconstitutional for state elections. Congress reacted immediately by adopting the Twenty-sixth Amendment providing for eighteen-year-old eligibility in all elections.

Recent Supreme Court decisions have dealt with still other limitations on the franchise or access to the ballot. Historically, in this highly mobile country massive disfranchisement has been caused by state voting laws requiring residence in the state and county for a certain period of time. In *Dunn v. Blumstein* (1972) the Court struck down a one-year-in-state and three-months-in-county requirement, suggesting that thirty days ought to be sufficient for the administrative tasks involved in registering new residents.[2] However, efforts to have the Court declare unconstitutional another source of disfranchisement, namely, state laws depriving persons convicted of felonies of the right to vote, failed in *Richardson v. Ramirez* (1974).

Unreasonably high filing fees for candidates for public office were invalidated in *Bullock v. Carter* (1972), and *Lubin v. Panish* (1974) held that states must provide some alternate means of ballot access for indigents unable to pay even a reasonable fee. Unreasonable restrictions on the access of minor parties to the ballot in Illinois were held unconstitutional in *Moore v. Ogilvie* (1969), but *American Party of Texas v. White* (1974)

[2] *Marston v. Lewis* (1973) accepted a 50-day period, however.

upheld somewhat less burdensome requirements for minor parties and independent candidates.

FREEDOM OF EXPRESSION

The First Amendment is the basic constitutional charter of American civil liberties. It provides: "Congress shall make no law . . . abridging the freedom of speech, or of the press." On its face, this is a clear and absolute barrier to any congressional abridgment of these freedoms. But we are all familiar with situations in which speech is abridged or restrained, with common consent. One may not talk freely in a library reading room or during a church service or while a court is in session. There are rules of order governing legislative assemblies or public meetings that restrain two people from talking at the same time or that prevent speech irrelevant to the issue under discussion. One who talks another person into committing a crime is a guilty partner in that crime.

The "freedom of speech" is obviously not involved in such restrictions. This concept relates rather to the right of discussion of public issues, free from governmental restraint, in the press or in the normal channels of public contact. But even here there are times and circumstances when the government thinks it necessary to clamp down restraints on discussion or printing. During World War I, for example, Congress passed the Espionage and Sedition Acts under which a substantial number of persons were jailed for criticizing the war effort or hampering it in some way. The Supreme Court had to decide whether such punishment for speech offenses was permissible under the First Amendment.

The argument was that when words are used to accomplish illegal acts, such as inciting to violence or hindering recruiting, the words themselves become tainted with the illegality of the acts and can be punished. The problem is, how closely must the speech be related to the crime in order for the speech itself to become punishable? How clear must the purpose be to incite to crime?

Justice Oliver Wendell Holmes was the spokesman for the Court in its first encounters with these World War I cases, and he developed the famous "clear and present danger" test to measure the extent of the federal government's powers to punish the spoken or written word because of its connection with illegal action. He wrote:

> The question in every case is whether the words used are used in such circumstances and are of such a nature as to create a clear and present danger that they will bring about the substantive evils that Congress has a right to prevent. It is a question of proximity and degree.

During wartime, he added, many things that might be said in time of peace cannot be "endured."

Thus he argued in *Schenck v. United States* (1919) that persons mailing circulars to men urging them not to register for the draft could be punished. But he soon found other situations where he and Justice Brandeis disagreed with the rest of the Court on whether "clear and present danger" had been shown to exist. It became obvious that this test could give differing results, depending upon who was applying it, and in fact it kept no one out of jail during the post-World War I hysteria.

The First Amendment refers specifically to Congress, but in 1925 the Supreme Court took an extremely important step in expanding the constitutional protection of speech and press to cover action by the states as well. The Court held in *Gitlow v. New York* (1925) that the "liberty" which the Fourteenth Amendment protects against infringement by the states without due process includes the freedoms mentioned in the First Amendment. Thus the principles of the First Amendment achieved universal applicability in American government.

There are in general two ways in which governments may deny freedom of speech or press. The first is by censorship, that is, imposing in advance legal limits that prohibit or otherwise effectively restrain speaking or publishing. The second is by punishing persons because what they have actually said or printed is alleged to violate the law. Censorship, or prior restraint, is generally regarded as more dangerous to freedom of expression than subsequent punishment, and the American tradition has been strongly against censorship.

FREEDOM OF THE PRESS

There can be no censorship of print under the First Amendment. The federal and state governments cannot prevent a book or newspaper from being published; they cannot require that publishers secure a license in order to operate; they cannot levy special taxes that discriminate against publishing as compared with other businesses. The outstanding anticensorship decision is *Near v. Minnesota* (1931). A state statute provided that "malicious, scandalous, and defamatory" newspapers could be treated as public nuisances and enjoined from publication by court order. The Supreme Court by a vote of 5 to 4 held that this was "the essence of censorship."

In 1971 the government sought injunctions against the *New York Times* and the *Washington Post* to prevent their continuing publication of the so-called "Pentagon Papers." This was a 47-volume report, made at the direction of the Defense Department, as to how the United States became involved in the Vietnam War. The study was classified as secret, but copies were furnished to the press in violation of government security regulations by Daniel Ellsberg. Applying the constitutional rule forbidding prior restraint of the press, the Supreme Court by a vote of 6 to 3 in *New York Times v. United States* (1971) dissolved the lower court injunctions that had interrupted publications of the papers.[3]

[3]Ellsberg was subsequently prosecuted for espionage, theft, and conspiracy in what promised to provide a major test of the First Amendment and the government's right to control the flow of information to the public. But after 89 days the judge declared a mistrial and dismissed the charges because of massive misconduct by the government in connection with the case, including the breaking and entering of Ellsberg's psychiatrist's office by the White House "plumbers," which was a notorious incident in the Watergate scandals.

It is not only newspapers, periodicals, and books that are exempt from censorship. Anyone with a hand printing press is a publisher for the purposes of the First Amendment, with full rights not to be hampered by public officials. Circulation of handbills dealing with public issues cannot be prevented by the police or by city ordinance, the Supreme Court held in *Lovell v. Griffin* (1938).

Obviously, it does little good to print if the printed matter cannot be circulated. Congress has barred certain kinds of material from the mails, including lottery tickets, obscene literature (to be considered shortly), and foreign political propaganda. The Post Office first began to confiscate foreign propaganda about 1940, though it had no statutory authority to do so at that time. In 1962, Congress passed a statute specifically authorizing the Postmaster General to detain "communist political propaganda" and to deliver it only upon the addressee's request. In *Lamont v. Postmaster General* (1965), the Supreme Court declared this statute unconstitutional, holding that to force an addressee to request in writing that his mail be delivered was an abridgment of First Amendment rights.

An aspect of press freedom currently under examination is the right of the press to print information about pending criminal prosecutions or trials in progress. There is widespread concern that the right to fair criminal trials is being undermined by the freedom with which police and prosecutors make public, and the communications media circulate, evidence against suspects before their trials are held, thus making the task of securing an unbiased jury very difficult. In the notorious case of *Sheppard v. Maxwell* (1966), the Supreme Court reversed a murder conviction on the ground that the news media had "inflamed and prejudiced the public" and turned the trial into "bedlam." With the support of the American Bar Association, judges in a number of recent cases have imposed restraints (referred to as "gag orders" by the press) on the pretrial release by police or prosecutors of incriminating information concerning accused persons, but the press has insisted that full publicity about law-enforcement activities is protected by the First Amendment and is the best guarantee of fair trials.

Newsmen generally contend that press freedom requires recognition of "confidentiality," that is, the right to protect their news sources against government efforts to compel disclosure through grand jury investigations or in criminal trials. Many state laws recognize this right, at least to some degree, but in *Branzburg v. Hayes* (1972) the Supreme Court ruled 5 to 4 that newsmen had no First Amendment right to refuse to answer questions of grand juries.

LIBEL

Libel is the defamation of character by print or other visual presentation such as television. It has long been understood that false and malicious statements about an individual damage him in reputation and earning power and lay the publisher open to prosecution for libel. In the past, private defamation suits have generally been thought to present no substantial First Amendment problems. In 1952, the Supreme Court even upheld the constitutionality of an Illinois "group libel" law, under which the head of an anti-Negro organization was convicted of making defamatory comments about blacks in general.

However, courts can award compensation not only for actual damages to a person or his reputation, but also for punitive damages, which may be any amount the judge or jury decides to assess. For publishing an advertisement attacking the treatment of blacks by the police in Montgomery, Alabama, the *New York Times* became the target of libel suits demanding over $6 billion. The Supreme Court was understandably concerned about the impact of such suits on freedom of discussion, and in *New York Times v. Sullivan* (1964) ruled that "erroneous statements honestly made" cannot be punished as libel. The First Amendment guarantees that "debate on public issues should be uninhibited, robust and wide-open." Inevitably, in such debate there may be false statements, damaging to official reputations. But a public official can recover damages for a defamatory falsehood only if he can prove that the statement was made with "actual malice," that is, "with knowledge that is was false or with reckless disregard of whether it was false or not."

In 1967 the Supreme Court extended the *New York Times* rule from public officials to private individuals who were "public figures" and, as such, legitimate objects of public attention. Then, in *Rosenbloom v. Metromedia* (1971), the rule was further extended to private individuals who were not public figures. A dealer in nudist magazines, arrested but found innocent of obscenity charges in court, was held not to have been libeled by radio broadcasts referring to him as a "smut peddler."

Thus, private individuals seemed to have been left powerless to protect their reputations, but in 1974 the Court retreated from the *Rosenbloom* holding. *Gertz v. Robert Welch, Inc.* ruled that a Chicago lawyer had been libeled by a John Birch Society magazine which charged that he was part of a communist conspiracy to discredit the police. However, the Court went on to hold that unless there was malice, libel awards must be limited to compensation for actual injury to a person or his reputation, thus limiting any future punitive awards.

OBSCENITY

Obscenity, like libel, has long been punishable under state laws, and there is also the federal obscenity statute applying to the mails. It was not until 1957 that the Supreme Court gave serious attention to the obscenity problem. Then in *Roth v. United States* it upheld laws punishing obscenity on the ground that obscenity was "utterly without redeeming social importance" and so completely outside the area of "constitutionally protected speech."

The Court developed three tests for determining whether materials are obscene. First, the *Roth* test was whether "to the average person, applying contemporary community standards, the dominant theme of the material taken as a whole appeals to prurient interest." Second, *Manual Enter-*

prises v. Day (1962) added that the material must be "patently offensive," its indecency "self-demonstrating." Finally, in *Jacobellis v. Ohio* (1964) the Court recognized a third test, that "material dealing with sex in a manner that advocates ideas . . . or that has literary or scientific or artistic value or any other form of social importance" cannot be considered obscene.

In the 1966 *Fanny Hill* case, the Court held that a book must fail all three of these tests before it can be regarded as obscene. Since the trial court admitted that the book had "a modicum of social value," it could not be branded obscene.

These decisions seemed to establish that only "hard-core pornography" met the Court's obscenity tests. As Justice Stewart said, he could not define obscenity, but "I know it when I see it." The Court recognized, however, that the open display or easy availability of sexual materials, which its opinions had helped to bring about, would be offensive to many. Consequently, in *Ginzburg v. United States* (1966) it moved against the "sordid business of pandering," and in *Ginsberg v. New York* (1968) it upheld a state law forbidding the sale of obscene materials to juveniles. Again, a federal statute authorizing persons receiving obscene material in the mail to demand the removal of their names from the firm's mailing list was upheld in *Rowan v. Post Office Department* (1970).

A ruling by the Court in *Stanley v. Georgia* (1969) that a person has the right to possess pornographic material in the privacy of his home was at first thought to mean that the right to possess included the right to receive. But in two 1971 decisions the Court upheld the federal statute against sending obscenity through the mail and the right of customs officials to seize obscene materials being imported.

A substantial change in the Court's definition of obscenity occurred in 1973. In *Miller v. California* and several companion cases the Burger Court substituted for the permissive holdings of the Warren Court a new rule permitting findings of obscenity if the material lacked serious literary, artistic, political, or scientific value. The "patent offensiveness" test was restrained, but offensiveness was to be judged against local, not national, community standards.

The threat thus posed to national distribution of books or motion pictures was demonstrated when a Georgia jury held a widely acclaimed film obscene. The Supreme Court in *Jenkins v. Georgia* (1974) felt compelled to reverse the conviction, cautioning that *Miller* did not mean to give local juries unbridled discretion. However, the Court in *Jenkins* reasserted that juries could base their determinations of offensiveness on the prevailing moral standards of their communities, thus seeming to guarantee continuing confusion on legal tests for obscenity.

State or city censorship of motion pictures was at one time fairly common. That such censorship, requiring advance approval by a public board before a movie could be shown, was a clear case of prior restraint, the Supreme Court never directly held. However, in *Freedman v. Maryland* (1965) the Court ruled that film censorship was constitutional "only if it takes place under procedural safeguards designed to obviate the dangers of a censorship system" and specified procedures so strict as to make it very difficult for a censorship system to operate.

RESTRAINT OF SPEECH AND ASSEMBLY

Censorship of speech is just as bad in principle as censorship of the press; and it is only in unusual situations, in which the social setting of the speech is such as to threaten danger to the public order, that controls over speech may be constitutionally imposed. The use of public streets, sidewalks, or parks for speech purposes may of course create traffic problems or the potentiality of disturbances. Consequently, municipalities often require some system of advance notification of meetings in public places and the issuance of permits covering speaking there.

Such permit systems have been held constitutional by the Supreme Court provided they are administered under standards that prevent discrimination or discretion in the granting of applications. If permits are issued to some groups and not to others, that is not only interference with freedom of assembly but also a denial of equal protection of the laws. Sound amplification creates a different problem, and may make speech liable to control as a public nuisance and an invasion of privacy.

SPEECH AND BREACH OF THE PEACE

The freedom to speak, then, is generally protected from advance restrictions, but if speech results in disorder or unlawful action of some kind, the speaker may be liable to punishment. One of the most common problems is that speech may inflame tempers and lead to violence. Preservation of order is a prime responsibility of every community; and in all states there are statutes punishing breach of the peace, disorderly conduct, inciting to riot, and like offenses. Where speech is an element in such illegal actions, serious questions arise in balancing the right to speak against the necessity of maintaining public order.

The Supreme Court has worked out three tests to be applied in passing on the constitutionality of punishment for speech. First, is the speech of a type entitled to constitutional protection? In *Chaplinsky v. New Hampshire* (1942) a member of Jehovah's Witnesses had cursed a city marshal, calling him a "damned racketeer" and "a damned Fascist"; and he was convicted for using "offensive and derisive" names in public. The Supreme Court upheld the conviction, on the ground that insults and "fighting" words are "no essential part of any exposition of ideas, and are of such slight social value as a step to truth that any benefit that may be derived from them is clearly outweighed by the social interest in order and morality."

Subsequently, the Court has been less certain about the right to punish "fighting words." In *Gooding v. Wilson* (1972) the Court reversed the conviction of a black who used threatening language to a white police officer, on the ground that the Georgia statute making unlawful the use of "opprobrious words or abrusive language" was too vague and overbroad.

The recent Court has also tended to extend protection to the public use of language regarded as offensive because of its vulgarity. In *Cohen v. California* (1971) the Court voided the conviction of a young man who had been found guilty of breach of the peace because he wore in public a jacket bearing a four-letter word expressing his opposition to the draft. Justice Harlan pointed out that words have an "emotive" as well as a "cognitive" function, and suggested that the emotive role "may often be the more important element of the over-all message sought to be communicated." Most of the other currently popular vulgarisms have also been cleared by the Court of charges of offensiveness or obscenity.[4]

Second, does the ordinance or statute for violation of which the speaker is being punished validly recognize the constitutional necessity for protection of speech? In *Terminiello v. Chicago* (1949) the Court invalidated a breach of the peace conviction under an ordinance that made it unlawful to "stir the public to anger" or "invite dispute." The evils had to be greater than that to justify a speech conviction, the Court said. *Street v. New York* (1969) involved a state law punishing expression of contempt for the flag "by words or act," and the Court reversed the conviction because no law can constitutionally make it a crime merely to speak "defiant or contemptous words."

Third, did a clear and present danger of actual breach of the peace result from the speech? In answering this question, a reviewing court of necessity has the difficult task of evaluating the correctness of the judgment of the police officers or others on the scene as to the potentialities of the speech for causing violence. In *Feiner v. New York* (1951), the Supreme Court was unwilling to question the judgment of the police and the trial court; but later, in such decisions as *Edwards v. South Carolina* (1963) and *Cox v. Louisiana* (1965), it did substitute its judgment for theirs.

Two prosecutions for alleged speech offenses achieved great notoriety during the violent 1960s, those of Dr. Spock and the Chicago Seven. Both involved charges of conspiracy, which are more difficult to defend against than charges of individual wrongdoing, since a conspiracy to commit an illegal act is a crime even if the action never occurs. Dr. Benjamin Spock and three other opponents of the war in Vietnam were convicted in 1968 of conspiring to encourage resistance to the draft, but the convictions were reversed on appeal in 1969 for errors in the trial. The Chicago Seven were participants in the disorders at the 1968 Chicago Democratic convention and were charged with violation of the federal Anti-Riot Act which makes criminal the crossing of state lines to incite or participate in a riot. Five of the defendants were convicted after a very disorderly trial before Judge Julius Hoffman, but two were held innocent by the jury, and all seven were freed of the conspiracy charge. The Court of Appeals subsequently reversed the convictions for errors in the trial, but by a 2 to 1 vote upheld the constitutionality of the Anti-Riot Act.

[4]See, for example, *Papish v. Board of Curators of University of Missouri* (1973), and *Eaton v. City of Tulsa* (1974).

FREEDOM TO DEMONSTRATE

The organized demonstration, so characteristic of the civil rights movement in the 1960s and the peace movement in the 1970s, is a form of communication that almost necessarily involves serious impact on other community interests. Demonstrations nearly always take place in public areas—the streets, sidewalks, or parks. Demonstrators use public places because they want to make contact with the public. They want to bring their views to the attention of people who do not know about them, who have not asked to be informed concerning them, and who may well object to them. An organized demonstration on public streets or sidewalks is bound to interfere to some degree with the normal use of these public facilities. A parade or a picket line, with songs, slogans, and signs, is "speech," but it is also action. As the Supreme Court has put it, it is "speech *plus.*"

Because of these facts, it is clear that the community is justified in requiring advance notification and permits for demonstrations. The Supreme Court so held in *Cox v. New Hampshire* (1941), a case involving a group of Jehovah's Witnesses who had marched single file along city streets carrying placards to advertise a meeting, without securing the license required by state law for "parades or processions" in a public street. The Court upheld this statute as a reasonable police regulation, administered under proper safeguards.

In the civil rights case of *Cox v. Louisiana* (1965), Justice Arthur Goldberg reiterated the necessity of maintaining order and freedom of movement in the streets:

> One would not be justified in ignoring the familiar red light because this was thought to be a means of social protest. Nor could one, contrary to traffic regulations, insist upon a street meeting in the middle of Times Square at the rush hour as a form of freedom of speech or assembly. Governmental authorities have the duty and responsibility to keep their streets open and available for movement.

The difficulty with this principle is that governmental authorities may deny permits to use the streets on the pretext of preserving order and movement of traffic when they are really seeking to prevent or punish demonstrations by unpopular groups. In city after city, civil rights or peace groups were denied parade permits or arrested for parading without permits, as was Martin Luther King in Birmingham in 1963. But in many of these cases, state or lower federal courts intervened and, following the line laid down by the Supreme Court, insisted that the authorities recognize the rights of the demonstrators. King's famous march from Selma to Montgomery in 1965 to demonstrate for black suffrage required an order from a federal judge to override the refusal of Alabama authorities to permit the march. When permits for demonstrations at the Chicago Democratic convention in 1968 were denied by the city, no court intervened and, with no legitimate method of dissent, the protest escalated into a bloody confrontation between demonstrators and police.

Permit ordinances or statutes may be held unconstitutional if they are too restrictive to give the authorities too much discretionary power to deny permits, as in *Walker v. Birmingham* (1967). Demonstrations around the White House cannot be prohibited, though the route of the paraders and the time of the demonstration can be specified by the authorities. Court-houses are an exception, however. State and federal statutes prohibiting demonstrations around courthouses intended to influence pending trials have been upheld by the Supreme Court (*Cox v. Louisiana* [1965]).

Normally there is no right to go onto private property to demonstrate without permission. In 1968 the Supreme Court upheld picketing in the parking lot of a shopping center, which is technically private property but to which the public has free access. However, in a later case involving handbilling in a shopping center, *Lloyd v. Tanner Corp.* (1972), the Court held that property does not lose its private character merely because the public is invited to use it for designated purposes, and ruled that First Amendment rights do not override property rights where alternative avenues of communication exist.

If the police undertake to arrest demonstrators for breach of the peace or other unlawful acts, they must be able to prove their charges in court. Of course, if demonstrators obstruct traffic by lying down in the street or if they physically attack the officers or other persons, their conduct is clearly illegal. But more difficult problems arise when demonstrators simply disobey police orders to disperse. In *Brown v. Louisiana* (1966), five blacks walked into a segregated library, requested a book, and remained after the librarian had told them the book was not in the library and asked them to leave. No one else was in the library, and they stood quietly until the sheriff arrived and arrested them for breach of the peace. The Supreme Court by a vote of 5 to 4 held that their action did not amount to a violation of the breach of the peace law. However, in *Adderly v. Florida* (1966), the Court thought that a demonstration on jail property against segregation in the jail was punishable as breach of the peace.

When a hostile crowd has formed around demonstrators and violence seems likely, the police have a serious dilemma. Should they seek to preserve order by ending the demonstration and, if necessary, arresting the demonstrators? Or should they let the demonstration continue and seek to control the crowd, arresting the principal troublemakers if necessary? In *Edwards v. South Carolina* (1963), involving a demonstration by some 200 black students on the grounds of the state capitol, the Court reversed the convictions of the demonstrators who had defied police orders to disband, holding that there had been no sufficient danger of disorder to justify the police action. In 1965, Dick Gregory led a night-time march on the sidewalk in front of Mayor Richard Daley's home in a Chicago residential area, but his conviction for disorderly conduct was reversed by the Supreme Court since the only actual disorder had been committed by the angry white residents of the area.

An interesting form of "speech plus" is so-called symbolic speech, such as burning a flag or a draft card. Here action conveys an ideational message but more effectively than speech could. In *United States v. O'Brien* (1968), the Supreme Court rejected the symbolic speech claim and upheld a conviction for draft-card burning. However, a different form of symbolic speech was accepted in *Tinker v. Des Moines School District* (1969). School officials in Des Moines had forbidden pupils to wear black armbands symbolizing opposition to the Vietnam War; the Court ruled that "apprehension of disturbances is not enough to overcome the right to freedom of expression." In *Street v. New York* (1969) the Court appeared to assume that flag burning could be punished. But in *Smith v. Goguen* (1974) a conviction of a youth for wearing an American flag on the seat of his pants was reversed on the ground that the statute against treating the flag "contemptuously" was too vague.

DIRECT ACTION AND CIVIL DISOBEDIENCE

"Direct action" is a broad term covering a wide range of challenges to established laws or practices. Direct action may be nonviolent or violent. It may operate within legal limits, or it may intentionally violate the law. The purpose of direct action is to dramatize issues, to create trouble and expense for the community, and to compel the "establishment" and the "power structure" to enter into negotiations for correcting the conditions protested.

The direct action program led by Martin Luther King, Jr., was nonviolent and operated in large part through legal methods such as parades and demonstrations. His program, however, did include the violation of laws he regarded as unjust. He said: "I would agree with Saint Augustine that 'an unjust law is no law at all.' "

Civil disobedience is an extreme form of direct action. It involves deliberate violation of the law, but the violation is not necessarily limited to laws the protesters regard as unjust. Rather, practitioners of civil disobedience violate admittedly valid laws, such as traffic regulations, in order to dramatize their grievances by creating a maximum of confusion and danger for the community. Thoreau and Gandhi agreed that persons who engaged in civil disobedience should willingly accept punishment for their acts.

FREEDOM OF ASSOCIATION

There is no provision in the Constitution specifically protecting freedom of association, yet the right of individuals to organize into groups for political, economic, religious, or social purposes is universally recognized. The constitutional basis for this freedom derives from the right of assembly and the freedoms of speech, press, and religion. Of course associational freedom is not absolute for any group, but the liberal state seeks to encourage the maximum of group freedom compatible with the general welfare. Restrictions on associational freedom must meet stringent consitutional tests.

The recent experiences of two organizations can best illustrate the issues in this field. The Communist party and other communist-oriented organizations and their members have been subjected to a wide variety of restrictions and punishments. In *Whitney v. California* (1927) the Supreme Court upheld a state criminal syndicalism law under which merely assisting in the formation of a state Communist party was a criminal act. The federal government acted principally under the Smith Act of 1940, which punishes advocating or teaching the violent overthrow of any government in the United States or organizing or knowingly becoming a member of a group that so advocates.

The Supreme Court affirmed the constitutionality of this act in *Dennis v. United States* (1951), a case in which 11 leaders of the American Communist party were convicted for organizing and leading the party. The Court held that, so far as the communist threat was concerned, the clear and present danger test "cannot mean that before the Government may act, it must wait until the *putsch* is about to be executed, the plans have been laid and the signal is awaited." Ten years later, in a case involving an active Communist leader, the Court also upheld the Smith Act provision making "knowing" membership in an organization advocating the forcible overthrow of the government a crime.

On the other hand, in *Yates v. United States* (1957), the Court required such strict standards of proof that individual Communists were conspiring to advocate overthrow of the government that the Department of Justice was forced to abandon its effort to secure any more conspiracy convictions under the Smith Act.

A second statutory weapon against the Communist party was the Subversive Activities Control Act of 1950. This act ordered communist-action organizations to register with the Attorney General, and a special board was set up to determine which organizations should be required to register. Following issuance of such an order, the organization had to supply to the government complete information on its officers and finances, any mail or radio broadcasts it sends out had to be identified as communist propaganda, its members committed a crime if they applied for or used a United States passport, and there were various other consequences. The Supreme Court upheld the constitutionality of the registration requirement as applied to the Communist party in 1961 but refused to pass on the validity of any of the various sanctions against members of the party until they were actually applied. As it turned out, registration was never accomplished. The Supreme Court ruled in 1964 that it would constitute self-incrimination to compel anyone to register for the party.

The principal sanctions in the act against members of the Communist party were also struck down by the Court on the basis of the *Yates* principle that individuals cannot be punished for mere membership in the party but only on the basis of specific intent to commit unlawful acts. *Aptheker v. United States* (1964) and *United States v. Robel* (1967) held that Communists could not be forbidden to apply for passports or to work in defense plants. Then, in *Brandenburg v. Ohio* (1969), the Court held unconstitutional the Ohio criminal syndicalism law, overruling *Whitney v. California,* which had upheld an almost identical statute.

The Supreme Court thus restored freedom of association for the Communist party and accepted the broad right to advocate overthrow of the government as an abstract doctrine. The Communist party, which during the Cold War had been forced off the ballot in all states, reappeared, and in *Communist Party of Indiana v. Whitcomb* (1974) the Court invalidated a state law which required the party to file a loyalty oath as a condition of gaining a place on the ballot for its candidates.

The National Association for the Advancement of Colored People (NAACP) has also been subject to attack, but unlike the case of the Communist party, the Supreme Court completely protected its associational rights as a lawful organization with nonviolent goals. The pressure on the NAACP came from Southern states that resented the activities of this organization in promoting desegregation in the public schools. For example, Alabama ordered the NAACP to register as an out-of-state corporation and, among other records, to give the names and addresses of its members in the state. The organization produced all the information required except the names and addresses, refusing to provide them on the ground that the members would be subject to social and economic pressure or even to physical attacks. The Supreme Court unanimously ruled against Alabama, concluding that compelled disclosure of the membership lists could interfere with the rights of individuals to engage in lawful association in support of their common beliefs.

In *NAACP v. Button* (1963) the Court held that the soliciting and prosecution of test cases in the courts to establish the civil rights of blacks did not violate state laws against stirring up litigation. Again, in *Gibson v. Florida Legislative Investigation Committee* (1963), the Court upheld the refusal of an NAACP official to bring the organization's membership list to a hearing where he was to be asked about possible Communist activity in the group.

Radical student and black organizations have been subjected to various kinds of official harassment and surveillance; but prosecutions against their members have usually charged violation of regular criminal statutes, thus avoiding the constitutional problems that would be raised by punitive legislation aimed at the associational rights of these organizations.

FREEDOM OF RELIGION

Freedom to worship God according to the dictates of individual conscience was one of the dominant motives in the founding of the American Colonies, and it might have been expected that provisions guaranteeing that right would have an important place in the Constitution. In fact, the founders left the original document almost devoid of language on the relationships of government and religion. The sole exception was the provision of Article VI that "no religious test shall ever be required as a qualification to any office or public trust under the United States."

The adoption of the First Amendment repaired the omissions of the original Constitution. The language of the amendment was specifically limited to Congress, though many states had similar provisions in their own constitutions. In 1940, however, the Supreme Court held that the freedom of religion clause in the First Amendment had been extended to the states by the Fourteenth Amendment's guarantee of "liberty."

The same principles that prevent prior restraint of speech or press also apply to religious observances or practices. It is unconstitutional for a state to require religious or philanthropic groups to get the consent of a public official before soliciting for funds. Again, the Supreme Court has held that Jehovah's Witnesses, who sell their literature from door to door, cannot be required to pay the license taxes imposed on other peddlers, since this would be a restraint on a religious observance.

Oregon raised a fundamental issue of religious liberty in 1922 when the state adopted a compulsory education act requiring all children to attend public schools for the first eight grades. This law would have deprived parents of the option of sending their children to religious or other non-public schools. In *Pierce v. Society of Sisters* (1925) the Supreme Court unanimously held the law invalid. The Court has also ruled that public schools may not compel students to participate in the exercise of saluting the flag if they have religious or other objections to such a ceremony.

Of course, cliams of religious freedom cannot be used to justify violation of the criminal laws of the land. Thought and belief are protected, but actions or practices that are made criminal by law or are outrageously offensive to public morals are not rendered immune from punishment because of alleged religious motivation. Thus polygamy as practiced by members of the early Mormon Church was punished with the approval of the Supreme Court.

Laws requiring businesses to close on Sunday do not violate the religious freedom of Jewish merchants and others whose religion requires them to close their stores on a different day. In *Braunfeld v. Brown* (1961), the Court ruled that Sunday observance, while originally religiously motivated, had now become purely a secular device for providing a uniform day of rest. However, secular regulations that unintentionally cause a hardship to particular religious groups may be voided if the courts find that there are alternative means by which the legislative purposes can be secured. In *Sherbert v. Verner* (1963), the Supreme Court held that a Seventh Day Adventist who was out of work because her religion forbade her to work on Saturday and all available jobs required Saturday service, could not be denied unemployment compensation.

An even more significant recognition of a religious claim for special treatment came before the Court in *Wisconsin v. Yoder* (1972). The Amish object to sending their children to school beyond the eighth grade, contending that further education is unnecessary for their way of life and would subject their children to the perils of a secular society. Accepting the special situation of the Amish, the Court granted their right to exemption from the state compulsory education law.

The laws compelling military service have handled the problem of religious liberty by granting exemption to conscientious objectors to war and allowing them to render alternative service. However, these statutes have raised problems by recognizing only conscientious objection based on "religious training and belief." The Court in *United States v. Seeger* (1965) partially avoided the issue by interpreting the statutory language very broadly. In *Welsh v. United States* (1970), it went further and held that the Selective Service Act granted exemption to men with strong and sincere moral and ethical beliefs against war and that their conscientious scruples need not be religiously based. But *Gillette v. United States* (1971) held that Congress had not granted exemption to objectors to particular wars on nonreligious grounds, a position taken by many on the Vietnam war.

ESTABLISHMENT OF RELIGION

When the First Amendment forbade Congress to pass any law "respecting an establishment of religion," it outlawed any system of an established church such as still exists in England, where there is one official church entitled to public financial support. However, the essential features of this system had largely been eliminated in America by the time the First Amendment was adopted. There were various other forms of assistance to religion out of public funds, however, which the establishment provision was presumably intended to terminate.

Establishment issues have been raised periodically in American history over such matters as the official designation of Thanksgiving Day, the provision of chaplains for Congress and in the armed services, or compulsory chapel services at West Point and Annapolis. However, there was comparatively little discussion of the establishment clause by the Supreme Court until the issue was raised in *Everson v. Board of Education* (1947). Under authorization by the state, a New Jersey township had reimbursed parents of public and Catholic school pupils for the transportation of their children to school on regular public transportation. The Supreme Court agreed that the establishment clause applied to the states because of the Fourteenth Amendment, but by a 5 to 4 vote went on to uphold the payments to parents of parochial school students.

Justice Hugo Black, writing the majority opinion, attempted to formulate a statement of what the establishment clause had come to mean:

> Neither a state nor the Federal Government can set up a church. Neither can pass laws which aid one religion, aid all religions, or prefer one religion over another. Neither can force nor influence a person to go to or to remain away from church against his will or force him to profess a belief or disbelief in any religion. No person can be punished for entertaining or professing religious beliefs or disbeliefs, for church attendance or non-attendance. No tax in any amount, large or small, can be levied to support any religious activities or institutions, whatever they may be called, or whatever form they may adopt to teach or practice religion.

On the basis of these principles, Justice Black acknowledged that the New Jersey statute approached the verge of constitutional power. However, he was able to uphold transportation payment by regarding the law as "welfare legislation" the benefits of which should not be denied to any individuals "because of their faith, or lack of it." But Justice Wiley B. Rutledge, one of the dissenters, thought that transportation "is as essential to education as any other element," and added that if providing transportation to religious schools is merely "public welfare legislation," then there can be "no possible objection to more extensive support of religious education by New Jersey."

Religious exercises or training in the public schools have seemed to the Supreme Court to be clearly contrary to the establishment clause. The New York Board of Regents composed a short "nondenominational" prayer, which they recommended be said aloud by each public school class at the beginning of every school day. The schools that adopted this procedure did not require students to participate; those who preferred could stand mute or leave the room.

In *Engel v. Vitale* (1962) the Supreme Court with only one dissent held that this was clearly a "religious activity." Again, in two 1963 decisions the Court held that Bible reading or recitation of the Lord's Prayer as part of the opening exercises in public schools was unconstitutional.

Another establishment problem was raised for the Court by the various "released time" programs for providing religious education in connection with the public schools. In 1948, the Court passed on such a program in the schools of Champaign, Illinois, under which public school children, on consent of their parents, attended classes in Protestant, Catholic, or Jewish religious instruction during school hours and in the school buildings. The religious teachers were not paid by the schools but were under the supervision of the school superintendents, and attendance was compulsory for participants in the program. The Court, with only one dissent, held this arrangement unconstitutional since tax-supported school buildings were being used in propagating religious doctrines, and the public school machinery was being employed to provide pupils for religious classes.

This decision was widely attacked in church circles, and the criticism apparently had some effect. Four years later the Court modified its stand and approved a New York City released time program that differed from the Campaign plan in that the instruction took place off the school premises.

Public financial aid to religious schools has been a key problem in congressional discussions of federal aid to education. In 1961, President Kennedy's educational bill failed of enactment because of this problem. But President Johnson successfully bypassed the religious school issue and secured passage of the Education Act of 1965 by directing the financial assistance primarily to children in poverty-impacted areas.

All of the funds provided under the 1965 act go to public school districts to meet the special educational needs of educationally deprived children, but through "shared time" or "dual enrollment" programs eligible children attending nonpublic schools also participate in these benefits. Thus federal funds are used to bear part of the cost of educating pupils of religious schools, and decisions of public school authorities may be affected by the necessity of accommodating their programs to those of religious schools. An eventual court test of the constitutionality of the 1965 act was made possible by the decision in *Flast v. Cohen,* already noted. But in *Wheeler v. Barrera* (1974) the Court avoided deciding whether the 1965 act required employment of teachers for special programs in private schools if such services were provided for public schools, or whether such a requirement, if it existed, would violate the First Amendment.

Most state efforts to give financial support to hard-pressed religious schools have been invalidated by the Supreme Court. In *Board of Education v. Allen* (1968) the Court upheld a New York law under which textbooks were provided to parochial as well as public school students, but in 1974 it disapproved a New Jersey program for reimbursing parents up to $20 for purchase of secular textbooks. A group of 1973 decisions, headed by *Committee for Public Education v. Nyquist,* struck down an assortment of state aid plans from New York and Pennsylvania, including state reimbursement or tax credits for tuition at parochial schools. Likewise *Lemon v. Kurtzman* (1971) ruled unconstitutional state grants to supplement the salaries of teachers of secular subjects in parochial schools, on the ground that this relationship would involve excessive "entanglement" of government and religion. However, federal and state building grants for construction of sectarian facilities at church-related colleges have been upheld as meeting the "no entanglement" test.

PROCEDURES IN CRIMINAL PROSECUTIONS

One of the basic concerns of the American Constitution is that persons shall not be deprived of life, liberty, or property without due process of law, which means a fair trial with all the procedural protections that have been developed in the Anglo-Saxon legal system. Half of the Bill of Rights—the Fourth through the Eighth Amendments—is devoted to stating the constitutional standards controlling criminal prosecutions, which indicates the importance these matters had in the eyes of the framers.

The Supreme Court ruled as early as 1833 that the protections of the Bill of Rights applied only against the national government, not the states. However, the Fourteenth Amendment adopted due process as a standard binding on the states, thus opening the way for Supreme Court review of state judicial proceedings. The Court's basic problem has been to determine whether the states should be required to observe the same court procedures that the Bill of Rights imposes in federal cases. For a long time, the Supreme Court considered "due process" as a comparatively loose requirement that permitted the states to adopt practices of criminal justice that would be unconstitutional if employed in federal courts. As Justice Benjamin N. Cardozo said in *Palko v. Connecticut* (1937), the states were free to adopt any standards so long as they were not in conflict with "the concept of ordered liberty," and did not violate principles of justice "so rooted in the traditions and conscience of our people as to be ranked as fundamental."

While this rule gave interesting recognition to the diversities of American federalism, it did create two major difficulties. One was the problem for the Court itself of deciding just which procedures were necessary to ordered liberty and which ones might be ignored without denying equal justice under law. The second difficulty was the one of explaining to ordinary citizens, untrained in the intricacies of constitutional law, how it was that the American Constitution did not protect equally defendants in state and federal courts. How could one explain why a federal court had to appoint counsel for a defendant too poor to hire one, while a state court did not? How could it be justified that a defendant could be convicted in a state court on evidence that could not have been legally presented in a federal court?

The pressure of such anomalies eventually led the Court very largely to abandon the effort to apply differing constitutional tests to state and federal courts, as will be explained in the following discussion.

The Fourth Amendment protects the people in their "persons, houses, papers, and effects" from "unreasonable" searches and seizures. This provision gives effect to the ancient English maxim that a man's home is his castle. As the test of reasonableness, the Amendment relied primarily upon requirement of a search warrant, issued "upon probable cause, supported by oath or affirmation, and particularly describing the place to be searched, and the persons or things to be seized." Warrants must be obtained from judicial officers, who are expected to prevent overzealous or unjustified police action. Evidence of crime that is seized without warrant and without justification by the police cannot be used as evidence in a criminal prosecution. This is the so-called "exclusionary rule," announced by the Supreme Court in 1914 for federal prosecutions. In *Wolf v. Colorado* (1949) the Court held that, while the Fourth Amendment ban on unreasonable searches and seizures applied to the states, the exclusionary rule did not, which meant that evidence illegally secured could nonetheless be used to secure convictions in state courts. The difficulty of rationalizing the conflicting practices in federal and state courts ultimately led the Court in *Mapp v. Ohio* (1961) to apply the exclusionary rule to the states also.

Searches and seizures may be made without search warrants in connection with lawful arrest, and the test for a lawful arrest is "probable cause." Search of the person arrested can be undertaken to find concealed weapons or evidence of crime. Even when there is no probable cause for arrest, police may stop, question, and search the outer clothing of suspicious persons, the Court held in *Terry v. Ohio* (1968). When making a lawful but warrantless arrest in a house or office, the police can seize evidence of crime which is in plain sight, but cannot search the entire house, said the Court in *Chimel v. California* (1969), overruling several decisions to the contrary.

Searches and seizures involving automobiles constitute a special problem. Because of the mobility of autos, warrants are usually not required for a search, though there must be probable cause. In two 1973 cases the Court held that arrest for a traffic violation justified a complete search of the driver's person.

Wiretapping was held in *Olmstead v. United States* (1928) not to come under the search and seizure ban, since nothing tangible was seized and the wiretapping was usually done outside the living quarters of the victim. However, Congress in 1934 forbade use in court of evidence secured by wiretapping. Electronic surveillance (bugging) accomplished without use of telephone wires was not affected by the statute, and so bugging was valid under the *Olmstead* rule if no physical invasion of a protected area occurred in placing the bug.

The Supreme Court finally abandoned the *Olmstead* reasoning and ruled in *Katz v. United States* (1967) that the Fourth Amendment did apply to the search and seizure of words and that it protected persons, not places. In this case, federal agents had secured evidence against a gambler by putting a bug on top of a public telephone booth he was using to place bets. The Court concluded that even though Katz was in a public, glass-enclosed booth he was constitutionally entitled to make a private telephone call that would not be relayed to government agents.

The statutes of many states authorize wiretapping provided advance court permission is secured, something on the order of a search warrant procedure. In the *Katz* case, the Supreme Court upheld the constitutionality of such an arrangement, and Congress promptly wrote this authority into the Omnibus Crime Control Act of 1968. President Nixon's first Attorney General, John N. Mitchell, on taking office in 1969 announced that he would use court-approved wiretaps in national security and organized crime cases. In addition, he contended that the government had unlimited power to eavesdrop on domestic organizations suspected of subversion, and in fact the White House did order wiretaps on thirteen government officials and four newsmen in an effort to check leaks of foreign policy information. The Supreme Court unanimously rejected Mitchell's position in 1972, and the unauthorized wiretapping was one of the abuses of power cited in the second article of impeachment against President Nixon.

In spite of the *Katz* decision, the practice of "third-party bugging" was upheld in *United States v. White* (1971). Here incriminating evidence of narcotics violations was secured by government agents by means of a transmitter which an informer had consented to wear on his person during conversations with the suspect, who of course was unaware that his words were being heard by third parties.

An important provision in the Fifth Amendment is that no one "shall be compelled in any criminal case to be a witness against himself." This protection embodies a basic principle of Anglo-Saxon jurisprudence that individuals are not obliged to help the government prove them guilty of crime. In *Malloy v. Hogan* (1964) the Court held that this provision also applies in state prosecutions.

The ban on self-incrimination means that defendants in criminal cases cannot be required to testify, and the judge cannot comment to the jury on their failure to take the witness stand. The protection covers also witnesses before congressional committees and grand juries. Persons "taking the Fifth" cannot be punished by loss of public jobs or disbarment from a profession. However, witnesses whose testimony is wanted can be granted immunity from prosecution for any criminal acts they may reveal, and then they are obliged to testify, and can be punished for contempt if they refuse. So-called "transactional immunity" bars subsequent prosecution for any transaction or matter concerning which the witness may testify. But the Organized Crime Control Act of 1970 authorized a more limited "testimonial immunity," under which the government can prosecute for criminal acts testified to if it can secure independent evidence of the crime.

The Fifth Amendment requires indictment by grand jury for capital or "otherwise infamous" crimes. This is a restraint on prosecuting officials, who must convince a citizen jury that there is substantial evidence of crime before a prosecution can be brought. It is generally true, however, that prosecutors dominate the grand jury and determine what evidence they will hear. The states are not bound by the grand jury requirement.

The defendant in a criminal trial is guaranteed a jury trial by the Sixth Amendment, a guarantee extended to the states by *Duncan v. Louisiana* (1968) for "serious" crimes, that is, those for which the statutory punishment is six months or longer. However, the familiar common-law, twelve-person, unanimous-verdict jury is under pressure. State criminal juries can now consist of as few as six persons, and the Supreme Court has upheld state laws providing for less-than-unanimous verdicts in criminal trials. In *Johnson v. Louisiana* (1972) a 9 to 3 verdict was upheld.

The Sixth Amendment also guarantees the assistance of legal counsel. In 1938 the Supreme Court ruled that defendants who could not afford to hire counsel must have counsel supplied for them, and in the famous case of *Gideon v. Wainwright* (1963) this rule was extended to state trials also.

Almost immediately the Court pushed the counsel requirement even further. In *Escobedo v. Illinois* (1964), a murder suspect being held by the police for questioning was denied the right to consult his lawyer, who was in the next room. The Court held that whenever a police investigation ceases to be general and focuses on a particular suspect, he is entitled to the assistance of counsel; and a subsequent conviction is invalid if he is denied access to counsel at the investigation stage.

This decision set off a national debate as to whether the police would ever be able to get any confessions under these restrictions. Undeterred by the controversy, the Supreme Court in *Miranda v. Arizona* (1966) expanded the *Escobedo* ruling into a general code of conduct for police interrogation. A suspect held in custody for questioning must be informed that he has the right to remain silent and warned that anything that he says can and may be used against him in court. He must be given the right to consult with an attorney before questioning and to have the attorney present during questioning if he desires. If the accused is unable to secure a lawyer, the Court added, one would have to be provided for him. If interrogation goes on without the presence of counsel and a confession is secured, the Court warned that a heavy burden would rest on the state to demonstrate that the defendant had knowingly and intelligently waived his privilege against self-incrimination and his right to retained or appointed counsel.

These decisions led to severe attacks on the Supreme Court for "coddling criminals" and making the law-enforcement task more difficult. Richard Nixon criticized the Court on this issue in his 1968 campaign, and the Crime Control Act of 1968 sought to reverse several of the Court's rulings. Actually, experience showed that the *Miranda* warnings did not materially affect the ability of the police to secure confessions.

The Burger Court, as expected, made some modifications in the criminal justice rulings of the Warren Court. In several cases it eased the *Miranda* requirements and limited the protection of the exclusionary rule. On the other hand, the *Gideon* holding on right to counsel was extended to misdemeanors as well as felonies, and in *Furman v. Georgia* (1972) the Court, over the dissent of the four Nixon appointees, took the momentous step of holding that capital punishment had been meted out at best so haphazardly and at worst so discriminatorily as to constitute cruel and unusual punishment, forbidden by the Eighth Amendment. Following that decision many states redrafted their statutes to make capital punishment mandatory for specified crimes, hoping in this way to meet the Supreme Court's objections.

EQUAL PROTECTION OF THE LAWS

Equal protection of the laws is an obligation imposed on the states by the Fourteenth Amendment, but in fact it is inherent in the concept of due process and so is binding on the federal government also. The principle of equal protection does not mean that all class legislation or legal discrimination is invalid. Men can be drafted into military service, but women are not; aliens have different obligations from citizens; large employers can be regulated differently from small employers; property in one section of a city can be zoned for uses forbidden in other sections of the city. But what equal protection does demand is that all persons in the same situation have the same privileges and be subject to the same legal obligations.

The equal protection clause has had a long history of use in testing economic and commercial regulations, but its greatest significance has been to protect against racial discrimination. The Fourteenth Amendment was adopted primarily to safeguard the rights of the newly freed blacks after the Civil War, though of course it did not attain, nor has it yet attained, that goal. Racial discrimination is not something that can be abolished by constitutional provision or judicial fiat. But the equal protection standard has been the foundation for increasingly important judicial pressure toward that goal.

The Civil Rights Act of 1875 forbade racial separation or discrimination in public conveyances, hotels, and theaters. However, the Supreme Court held this law unconstitutional in the *Civil Rights Cases* (1883), on the ground that the Fourteenth Amendment did not apply to discrimination by private individuals or business corporations; it forbade only *state* (i.e., official or governmental) action of a discriminatory nature.

In spite of this serious setback, there were a few favorable Supreme Court rulings over the years. In 1886, the Court struck down a San Francisco ordinance which, under the guise of a safety regulation, was actually aimed at Chinese laundries. In 1935, the Court took note of the fact that no black had ever been called for jury duty in a particular Alabama county and gave notice that it would void criminal convictions of blacks obtained under those conditions. In 1948, the Court held that state courts would violate the Fourteenth Amendment if they enforced restrictive convenants under which landowners agree among themselves not to sell their property to blacks or other minority racial groups.

By all odds the most significant judicial blow against racial discrimination was *Brown v. Board of Education* (1954), in which the Supreme Court held racial segregation in the public schools unconstitutional. The Court itself had created the principal legal argument in support of segregation in 1896, when it had ruled that segregating the races in interstate transportation was valid if equal accommodations were offered to both races. This doctrine of "separate but equal" was finally overruled in the *Brown* decision, the Court holding that segregated educational facilities, even though equal in their physical aspects, were "inherently unequal" and deprived the children of the minority group of equal educational opportunities.

Naturally, the Court was concerned about the problem of enforcing a ruling that demanded the abolition of passionately held social practices in whole sections of the country. After an additional hearing, the Court sent the cases that had been decided in *Brown* back to the federal district courts in which they had originated, and instructed the district judges to require local school boards to proceed with plans for desegregation "with all deliberate speed."

At first it seemed that the prestige of the Court might substantially temper the expected resistance to the decree. The Supreme Court may have expected that it would receive some support from Congress and the President in winning acceptance for its ruling, but no such aid was forthcoming. On the contrary, 96 Southern congressmen signed a manifesto in 1956 challenging the legality of the Court's decision, and President Eisenhower, while declaring that he would enforce the law, declined to attempt any organization of popular support for the desegregation ruling. Thus the responsibility for effecting this tremendous social revolution was left to some 58 federal district and court of appeals judges in the Southern states, many of whom were personally opposed to the principle of the *Brown* decision.

Under these circumstances, it was not surprising that progress toward the goal of desegregation was slow and uneven. In the border states a considerable measure of integration was achieved, but in the "old South" almost complete frustration of desegregation efforts was achieved by a variety of methods. The most publicized resistance was that organized by legislation in Virginia, and the violence associated with integration of the Little Rock high school in Arkansas.

This experience demonstrated that school integration could never be achieved by lawsuits alone. The support and participation of the political branches of the government was necessary. Belatedly, the President and Congress assumed their responsibilities for carrying through the revolution that the Supreme Court had begun. In the fall of 1962, President Kennedy had to send federal marshals and troops to enforce a court order to admit a black student to the University of Mississippi. After police dogs, cattle prods, and fire hoses had been used against demonstrating blacks in Birmingham in 1963, President Kennedy proposed new federal civil rights legislation. Following his assassination, President Johnson made adoption of the Kennedy civil rights bill one of his primary purposes, and a bipartisan majority in Congress passed the Civil Rights Act of 1964. This statute authorized the Attorney General to bring school desegregation suits in the name of the United States, a power that Congress had refused to provide in the Civil Rights Act of 1957.

The 1964 act also included a general provision prohibiting racial discrimination in any local program receiving federal financial assistance. This sanction became of very great importance in 1965, when Congress adopted President Johnson's plan for federal financial assistance to primary and secondary schools. To become eligible for these grants in the fall of 1965, all public schools had to certify that they were integrated or file acceptable plans for achieving complete integration. The federal Office of Education issued guidelines requiring significant progress toward desegregation from year to year as a condition of receiving federal aid; and the Supreme Court applied additional pressure in 1968 by holding "freedom of choice" plans, which were a principal Southern resistance device, unconstitutional when such plans did not actually promote desegregation. The Nixon administration brought some relaxation in federal pressure toward achievement of desegregation, but initial efforts by the Justice Department to have the Supreme Court modify its position failed.

By 1972 court-ordered busing of children out of their neighborhood to achieve integration was developing into a major political issue. A new factor was that Northern cities were being affected. Segregation in the North was usually de facto, the result not of laws or school policies but of ghetto housing barriers which created all-black neighborhood schools. In 1972 President Nixon called on Congress unsuccessfully for legislation which would halt, delay, or minimize court-ordered busing. But the next year the Supreme Court, which for almost 20 years had been unanimous in support of desegregation measures, split 4 to 4 on a city-county integration plan for the schools of the Richmond, Virginia, area. Then in *Milliken v. Bradley* (1974) the Court by a 5 to 4 vote held that the white suburban school districts outside Detroit should not be forced to integrate with the city's predominantly black schools by court-ordered busing across city-county boundaries. This decision, which was almost certain to assure the continuance of all-black central city schools, took the pressure off Congress, where the House and Senate had been at odds over antibusing provisions in the 25-billion-dollar Education Act of 1974. As passed the act forbade the use of federal school funds to finance busing for desegregation, allowed courts to terminate busing in cases where a school was able to show it had desegregated, and banned court-ordered busing past a student's second nearest school unless a court found that this ban violated the constitutional rights of minority children.

As already noted, the *Civil Rights Cases* (1883) held that the equal protection clause applied only to state action, not to private discrimination. However, private discrimination has in fact been outlawed in many situations. A major development was the Civil Rights Act of 1964, which made unlawful racial discrimination in "public accommodations" such as restaurants, hotels, motels, and bus stations. This statute grew out of the sit-in technique employed by the civil rights movement in the early 1960s.

Blacks would take seats at "white only" lunch counters and, after being refused service, continue to sit there until arrested or ousted by force. They were customarily charged either with breach of the peace or criminal trespass (i.e., remaining on private property after being requested to leave).

While the Supreme Court considered a number of sit-in cases between 1961 and 1964, it never found a case that would require it to pass squarely on the constitutional situation of sit-in trespassers. If such a case had arisen, the Court would have had to balance the rights of a restaurant owner to choose his customers against the right of any respectable person able to pay for service to enter a place of public accommodation and be served.

The nature of the legal problem was changed when Congress, acting under its power to regulate interstate commerce and facilities used by travelers in interstate commerce, passed the 1964 act which made refusal of service for racial reasons unlawful conduct. The act was promptly upheld by the Supreme Court in *Heart of Atlanta Motel v. United States* (1964).

Private discrimination has also become subject to constitutional restraint by expansion of the "state action" concept. For example, restrictive covenants, under which private property owners agree with each other not to sell their houses to specified racial groups, were rendered useless when in *Shelley v. Kraemer* (1948) the Supreme Court held that enforcement of the covenants by courts would constitute "state action" forbidden by the Fourteenth Amendment.

Private clubs may discriminate in choosing their membership, but they must be truly "private." The case of *Daniel v. Paul* (1969) involved a segregated amusement center in Arkansas which claimed to be a private club but sold "memberships" for 25 cents; it was ordered to admit blacks. The same result was reached in *Sullivan v. Little Hunting Park* (1969), a case in which a housing development operating a community swimming pool had practiced racial exclusion. But *Moose Lodge v. Irvis* (1972) involved what was clearly a private club with a whites-only membership policy. The Court held that the fact that the state had granted a liquor license to the club did not bring the club under the "state action" rule.

The legal right of open access to housing has been firmly established, even though the actuality has been far from achieved. Initially "open occupancy" laws, requiring owners of property or real estate agents to offer housing for rent or sale without racial restrictions, were adopted in numerous states and cities, usually after bitter controversy. In California, such a law was repealed in 1964 by a popular referendum, but in 1966 the state supreme court held the repeal unconstitutional as a denial of equal protection of the laws, and the Supreme Court agreed in *Reitman v. Mulkey* (1967).

National action against discrimination in housing came in 1968. Following the assassination of Martin Luther King, Jr., Congress passed a civil rights act containing open-housing provisions applicable to a broad range of discriminatory practices. A few weeks later, the Supreme Court in *Jones v. Alfred H. Mayer Co.* ruled that a provision of the Civil Rights Act of 1866, although never before interpreted so broadly, had made illegal every racially motivated refusal by property owners to rent or sell.

NONRACIAL DISCRIMINATION

Equal protection has increasingly been invoked to challenge the legality of nonracial classifications. Congress required equal pay for women in 1963, and the Civil Rights Act of 1964 banned discrimination in employment on the basis of sex as well as race or religion. A constitutional amendment removing all legal disabilities based on sex was adopted by Congress in 1972, and in 1975 lacked only affirmative action by 4 state legislatures to become the Twenty-Seventh Amendment.

Beginning in 1971, the Supreme Court undertook to invalidate some long-established sexual discriminations, but refused to go so far as to establish sex as a "suspect classification" like race. For example, in 1974 the Court upheld a Florida law giving widows, but not widowers, a property tax exemption, on the ground that widows were more likely to be in financial straits.

Extension of the equal protection concept into new fields is related to changing perceptions of "fundamental rights." We have already seen how the right to counsel and access to the courts have been held to be fundamental rights which must not be denied to those unable to pay for them. In a significant line of decisions the recent Court has considered the legal situation of illegitimate children, and has concluded that they have some fundamental rights which cannot be infringed by state legislation.

Again, the right to travel from state to state, while long recognized, has been used in new situations, as in striking down state laws requiring indigents to live in a state for one year before becoming eligible for welfare payments. The argument that education is a fundamental right, and that equal protection is denied by a system of financial support geared to widely varying property tax bases, was accepted by the Supreme Court of California in 1972 but rejected by the U.S. Supreme Court in *San Antonio School District v. Rodriquez* (1973).

PROTECTION OF PROPERTY RIGHTS

By a variety of provisions, the Constitution protects private property rights against government action. Both federal and state governments have the power of eminent domain, that is, to take private property that is needed for a public purpose. But the Fifth Amendment requires Congress to give "just compensation" for property so taken, and the states have the same obligation under the due process clause.

The states are forbidden by Article 1, section 10, to pass any law "impairing the obligation of contracts." In the first half of the nineteenth century, the contract clause was the principal guarantee against public regulation, particularly since Chief Justice Marshall interpreted the clause to cover charters granted to corporations. But the present-day significance of the contract clause is not great.

The most general protection for property rights is found in the due process clauses of the Fifth and Fourteenth Amendments. Beginning in the 1880s the Supreme Court developed a very strong laissez faire bias in applying the due process test to state economic legislation. Among the important decisions striking down state regulation of private enterprise were *Lochner v. New York* (1905), in which a state 10-hour law for bakers was declared unconstitutional, and *Adkins v. Children's Hosptial* (1923), voiding a District of Columbia minimum wage law for women. The Court was also during this period quite unfriendly to price control legislation. However, in 1934 the Court admitted that the states could regulate the price of milk; and in 1937 state minimum wage laws were approved. Since that time the Court has almost never struck down economic regulatory legislation, either federal or state, on due process grounds.

THE RIGHT TO PRIVACY

The Constitution protects privacy of the home by the Fourth Amendment's provision against unreasonable searches and seizures, but modern technology and the conditions of living in a mass society have made invasion of privacy increasingly common. The Supreme Court took an important step toward recognizing a general constitutionally protected right of privacy in *Griswold v. Connecticut* (1965) when it held unconstitutional a state statute forbidding the use of birth control devices. In the marriage relationship, wrote Justice William O. Douglas, "we deal with a right of privacy older than the Bill of Rights."

In two sensational 1973 decisions, *Roe v. Wade* and *Doe v. Bolton,* the Court invoked the right of privacy in holding unconstitutional the criminal abortion laws of two states, and announced guidelines limiting the power of the states to regulate abortion. The Court held in a 7 to 2 decision that during the first three months of pregnancy the decision to have an abortion must be left entirely to the woman and her physician. During the second trimester the state can set standards for the conditions under which abortions are performed, in the interest of preserving the health of the mother or the potential life of the unborn infant. In the third trimester the state, to safeguard the unborn infant, can ban all abortions except those performed to save the mother's life. The Court declined to find that the word "person" as it appears in the equal protection clause includes unborn children. These rulings were highly controversial, and efforts were immediately untertaken in Congress to secure a constitutional amendment forbidding abortion except in medical emergencies where the life of the mother was threatened.

SUMMARY

The maintenance of political and civil liberties is an indispensable condition to the successful operation of a democratic form of government. These liberties have a firm foundation in the American Constitution, but it requires more than words on parchment to give them reality. First of all, citizens must be able to defend their rights at the ballot box. The limitations on Negro voting in many states long supported racial discrimination in other fields. With the vote, any group is in a position to defend its own rights.

Second, defense of individual liberties requires action by the courts. They must interpret the established constitutional principles and apply them to the constantly new problems of suppression or discrimination that arise. They must be strong enough to defend the constitutional freedoms of unpopular persons.

Third, the principles of an open society must be generally accepted. It has taken many centuries to develop such concepts as due process of law, equal protection of the laws, freedom of speech and press, and the guarantee against taking of property without just compensation. In times of stress there are always temptations to abandon the rule of law and to revert to the methods of direct action or revenge or violence. The Constitution has provided a worthy guide for American democracy in both good and bad times.

REVIEW QUESTIONS

1 How does the Constitution guarantee the right to vote?

2 What is the present status of the poll tax as a prerequisite for voting?

3 How did the Voting Rights Act of 1965 undertake to guarantee Negroes access to the ballot?

4 What is the purpose of the "clear and present danger" test?

5 Why has censorship been regarded as such a serious form of limitation on expression of opinion?

6 What is the nature of the danger to free expression resulting from prosecutions for libel?

7 What is the constitutional justification for actions taken by Congress against the Communist Party?

8 How have the protections of the First Amendment, which applies specifically to Congress, been made applicable to the states?

9 What limits has the Supreme Court appeared to set on public financial aid to church schools or religious programs in public schools?

10 What have been the problems in enforcement of the Supreme Court's decision declaring segregation in the public schools unconstitutional?

FOR FURTHER READING

Abraham, Henry J.: *Freedom and the Court: Civil Rights and Liberties in the United States,* Oxford University Press, New York, 1972.

Bailey, Stephen K.: *Congress in the Seventies,* St. Martin's Press, New York, 1970.

Barber, James David (ed.): *Choosing the President,* Prentice-Hall, Inc., Englewood Cliffs, N.J., 1974.

Berger, Raoul: *Executive Privilege: A Constitutional Myth,* Harvard University Press, Cambridge, Mass., 1974.

————: *Impeachment: The Constitutional Problems,* Harvard University Press, Cambridge, Mass., 1973.

Bickel, Alexander M.: *The Least Dangerous Branch,* The Bobbs-Merrill Company, Inc., Indianapolis, 1962.

————: *The Supreme Court and the Idea of Progress,* Harper & Row, Publishers, Incorporated, New York, 1970.

Black, Charles L., Jr.: *Impeachment: A Handbook,* Yale University Press, New Haven, Conn., 1974.

Clor, Harry: *Obscenity and Public Morality,* The University of Chicago Press, Chicago, 1969.

Corwin, Edward S.: *The President: Office and Powers,* 4th ed., New York University Press, New York, 1957.

Dixon, Robert G., Jr.: *Democratic Representation: Reapportionment in Law and Politics,* Oxford University Press, New York, 1968.

Dorsen, Norman (ed.): *The Rights of Americans,* Pantheon Books, New York, 1972.

Emerson, Thomas I.: *The System of Freedom of Expression,* Random House, Inc., New York, 1970.

Fisher, Louis: *President and Congress: Power and Policy,* The Free Press, New York, 1972.

Freund, Paul A.: *The Supreme Court of the United States,* The World Publishing Company, Cleveland, 1961.

Goldwin, Robert A. (ed.): *A Nation of States,* Rand McNally & Company, Chicago, 1963.

Hardin, Charles M.: *Presidential Power and Accountability: Toward a New Constitution,* The University of Chicago Press, Chicago, 1974.

Hughes, Charles Evans: *The Supreme Court of the United States,* Columbia University Press, New York, 1928.

Kallenbach, Joseph E.: *The American Chief Executive,* Harper & Row, Publishers, Incorporated, New York, 1966.

Kalven, Harry, Jr.: *The Negro and the First Amendment,* The University of Chicago Press, Chicago, 1966.

Koenig, Louis W.: *The Chief Executive,* Harcourt, Brace & World, Inc., New York, 1968.

Kurland, Philip B.: *Politics, the Constitution, and the Warren Court,* The University of Chicago Press, Chicago, 1970.

―――― (ed.): *Supreme Court Review,* The University of Chicago Press, Chicago, 1960–1974.

Lewis, Anthony: *Gideon's Trumpet,* Random House, Inc., New York, 1964.

McCloskey, Robert G.: *The American Supreme Court,* The University of Chicago Press, Chicago, 1960.

Mason, Alpheus T., and William M. Beaney: *The Supreme Court in a Free Society,* W. W. Norton & Company, Inc., New York, 1968.

Mitford, Jessica: *The Trial of Dr. Spock,* Alfred A. Knopf, Inc., New York, 1969.

Murphy, Walter F.: *Congress and the Court,* The University of Chicago Press, Chicago, 1962.

Neustadt, Richard E.: *Presidential Power,* John Wiley & Sons, Inc., New York, 1960.

Peirce, Neal R.: *The People's President: The Electoral College in American History,* Simon and Schuster, Inc., New York, 1968.

Peltason, Jack: *Fifty-Eight Lonely Men: Southern Federal Judges and School Desegregation,* Harcourt, Brace & World, Inc., New York, 1961.

Pritchett, C. Herman: *The American Constitution,* 2d ed., McGraw-Hill Book Company, New York, 1968.

―――――: *The Roosevelt Court,* Quadrangle Books, Inc., Chicago, 1969.

Rossiter, Clinton: *The American Presidency,* Harcourt, Brace & World, Inc., New York, 1960.

Sayre, Wallace, and Judith H. Parris: *Voting for President,* The Brookings Institution, Washington, D.C., 1970.

Schlesinger, Arthur M., Jr.: *The Imperial Presidency,* Houghton Mifflin Company, Boston, 1973.

Shapiro, Martin: *Freedom of Speech: The Supreme Court and Judicial Review,* Prentice-Hall, Inc., Englewood Cliffs, N.J., 1966.

―――――: *Law and Politics in the Supreme Court,* The Free Press, New York, 1964.

Swindler, William F.: *Court and Constitution in the Twentieth Century: The New Legality, 1932–1968,* The Bobbs-Merrill Company, Inc., Indianapolis, 1970.

Tugwell, Rexford G., and Thomas E. Cronin (eds.): *The Presidency Reappraised,* Praeger Publishers, New York, 1974.

Warren, Charles: *The Supreme Court in United States History,* 2 vols., Little, Brown and Company, Boston, 1947.

APPENDIX

CONSTITUTION OF THE UNITED STATES OF AMERICA

We the people of the United States, in Order to form a more perfect Union, establish Justice, insure domestic Tranquility, provide for the common defence, promote the general Welfare, and secure the Blessings of Liberty to ourselves and our Posterity, do ordain and establish this CONSTITUTION for the United States of America.

ARTICLE I

Section 1 All legislative Powers herein granted shall be vested in a Congress of the United States, which shall consist of a Senate and House of Representatives.

Section 2 *1* The House of Representatives shall be composed of Members chosen every second Year by the People of the several States, and the Electors in each State shall have the Qualifications requisite for Electors of the most numerous Branch of the State Legislature.

2 No Person shall be a Representative who shall not have attained to the Age of twenty five Years, and been seven Years a Citizen of the United States, and who shall not, when elected, be an Inhabitant of that State in which he shall be chosen.

3 Representatives and direct Taxes[1] shall be apportioned among the several States which may be included within this Union according to their respective Numbers, which shall be determined by adding to the whole Number of free Persons, including those bound to Service for a Term of Years, and excluding Indians not taxed, three fifths of all other Persons.[2] The actual Enumeration shall be made within three Years after the first Meeting of the Congress of the United States, and within every subsequent Term of ten Years, in such Manner as they shall by Law direct. The Number of Representatives shall not exceed one for every thirty Thousand, but each State shall have at Least one Representative; and until such enumeration shall be made, the State of New Hampshire shall be entitled to chuse three, Massachusetts eight, Rhode-Island and Provi-

---

[1] Modified as to direct taxes by the Sixteenth Amendment.
[2] Replaced by the Fourteenth Amendment.

dence Plantations one, Connecticut five, New-York six, New Jersey four, Pennsylvania eight, Delaware one, Maryland six, Virginia ten, North Carolina five, South Carolina, five, and Georgia three.

4 When vacancies happen in the Representation from any State, the Executive Authority thereof shall issue Writs of Election to fill such Vacancies.

5 The House of Representatives shall chuse their Speaker and other Officers; and shall have the sole Power of Impeachment.

Section 3 *1* The Senate of the United States shall be composed of two Senators from each State, chosen by the Legislature thereof,[3] for six Years; and each Senator shall have one Vote.

2 Immediately after they shall be assembled in Consequence of the first Election, they shall be divided as equally as may be into three Classes. The Seats of the Senators of the first Class shall be vacated at the Expiration of the second Year, of the second Class at the Expiration of the fourth Year, and of the third Class at the Expiration of the sixth Year, so that one third may be chosen every second Year; and if Vacancies happen by Resignation, or otherwise, during the Recess of the Legislature of any State, the Executive thereof may make temporary Appointments until the next Meeting of the Legislature, which shall then fill such Vacancies.

3 No Person shall be a Senator who shall not have attained to the Age of thirty Years, and been nine Years a Citizen of the United States, and who shall not, when elected, be an Inhabitant of that State for which he shall be chosen.

4 The Vice President of the United States shall be President of the Senate, but shall have no Vote, unless they be equally divided.

5 The Senate shall chuse their other Officers, and also a President pro tempore, in the Absence of the Vice President, or when he shall exercise the Office of President of the United States.

6 The Senate shall have the sole Power to try all Impeachments. When sitting for that Purpose, they shall be on Oath or Affirmation. When the President of the United States is tried, the Chief Justice shall preside: And no Person shall be convicted without the Concurrence of two thirds of the Members present.

7 Judgment in Cases of Impeachment shall not extend further than to removal from office, and disqualification to hold and enjoy any Office of honor, Trust or Profit under the United States: but the Party convicted shall nevertheless be liable and subject to Indictment, Trial, Judgment and Punishment, according to Law.

Section 4 *1* The Times, Places and Manner of holding Elections for Senators and Representatives, shall be prescribed in each State by the Legislature thereof; but the Congress may at any time by Law make or alter such Regulations, except as to the Places of chusing Senators.

2 The Congress shall assemble at least once in every Year, and such Meeting shall be on the first Monday in December, unless they shall by Law appoint a different Day.[4]

[3] Modified by the Seventeenth Amendment.
[4] Modified by the Twentieth Amendment.

Section 5   *1* Each House shall be the Judge of the Elections, Returns and Qualifications of its own Members, and a Majority of each shall constitute a Quorum to do Business; but a smaller Number may adjourn from day to day, and may be authorized to compel the attendance of absent Members, in such Manner, and under such Penalties as each House may provide.

2 Each House may determine the Rules of its Proceedings, punish its Members for Disorderly Behaviour, and, with the Concurrence of two thirds, expel a Member.

3 Each House shall keep a Journal of its Proceedings, and from time to time publish the same, excepting such Parts as may in their Judgment require Secrecy; and the Yeas and Nays of the Members of either House on any question shall, at the Desire of one fifth of those Present, be entered on the Journal.

4 Neither House, during the Session of Congress, shall, without the Consent of the other, adjourn for more than three days, nor to any other Place than that in which the two Houses shall be sitting.

Section 6   *1* The Senators and Representatives shall receive a Compensation for their Services, to be ascertained by Law, and paid out of the Treasury of the United States. They shall in all Cases, except Treason, Felony and Breach of the Peace, be privileged from Arrest during their Attendance at the Session of their respective Houses, and in going to and returning from the same; and for any Speech or Debate in either House, they shall not be questioned in any other Place.

2 No Senator or Representative shall, during the Time for which he was elected, be appointed to any civil Office under the Authority of the United States, which shall have been created, or the Emoluments whereof shall have been encreased during such time; and no Person holding any Office under the United States, shall be a member of either House during his Continuance in Office.

Section 7   *1* All Bills for raising Revenue shall originate in the House of Representatives; but the Senate may propose or concur with Amendments as on other Bills.

2 Every Bill which shall have passed the House of Representatives and the Senate, shall, before it become a Law, be presented to the President of the United States; If he approve he shall sign it, but if not he shall return it, with his Objections to that House in which it shall have originated, who shall enter the Objections at large on their Journal, and proceed to reconsider it. If after such Reconsideration two thirds of that House shall agree to pass the Bill, it shall be sent, together with the Objections, to the other House, by which it shall likewise be reconsidered, and if approved by two thirds of that House, it shall become a Law. But in all such Cases the Votes of both Houses shall be determined by Yeas and Nays, and the Names of the Persons voting for and against the Bill shall be entered on the Journal of each House respectively. If any Bill shall not be returned by the President within ten Days (Sundays excepted) after it shall have been presented to him, the same shall be a Law, in like Manner as if he had signed it, unless the Congress by their Adjournment prevent its Return, in which Case it shall not be a Law.

3 Every Order, Resolution, or Vote to which the Concurrence of the Senate and House of Representatives may be necessary (except on a question of Adjournment) shall be presented to the President of the United States; and before the same shall take Effect, shall be approved by him, or being disapproved by him, shall be repassed by two thirds of the Senate and House of Representatives, according to the Rules and Limitations prescribed in the Case of a Bill.

General Welfare Clause

Section 8 The Congress shall have Power *1* To lay and collect Taxes, Duties, Imposts and Excises, to pay the Debts and provide for the common Defence and general Welfare of the United States; but all Duties, Imposts and Excises shall be uniform throughout the United States;

2 To borrow Money on the credit of the United States;

3 To regulate Commerce with foreign Nations, and among the several States, and with the Indian Tribes;

4 To establish an uniform Rule of Naturalization, and uniform Laws on the subject of Bankruptcies throughout the United States;

5 To coin Money, regulate the Value thereof, and of foreign Coin, and fix the Standard of Weights and Measures;

6 To provide for the Punishment of counterfeiting the Securities and current Coin of the United States;

7 To establish Post Offices and post Roads;

8 To promote the Progress of Science and useful Arts, by securing for limited Times to Authors and Inventors the exclusive Right to their respective Writings and Discoveries;

9 To constitute Tribunals inferior to the supreme Court;

10 To define and punish Piracies and Felonies committed on the high Seas, and Offences against the Law of Nations;

11 To declare War, grant Letters of Marque and Reprisal, and make Rules concerning Captures on Land and Water;

12 To raise and support Armies, but no Appropriation of Money to that Use shall be for a longer Term than two Years;

13 To provide and maintain a Navy;

14 To make Rules for the Government and Regulation of the land and naval Forces;

15 To provide for calling forth the Militia to execute the Laws of the Union, suppress Insurrections and repel Invasions;

16 To provide for organizing, arming, and disciplining, the Militia, and for governing such Part of them as may be employed in the Service of the United States, reserving to the States respectively, the Appointment of the Officers, and the Authority of training the Militia according to the discipline prescribed by Congress;

17 To exercise exclusive Legislation in all Cases whatsoever, over such District (not exceeding ten Miles square) as may, by Cession of particular States, and the Acceptance of Congress, become the Seat of the Government of the United States, and to exercise like Authority over all Places purchased by the Consent of the Legislature of the State in which the same shall be, for the Erection of Forts, Magazines, Arsenals, dock-Yards, and other needful Buildings;—And

18 To make all Laws which shall be necessary and proper for carrying into Execution the foregoing Powers, and all other Powers vested by this Constitution in the Government of the United States, or in any Department or Officer thereof.

Section 9   *1* The Migration or Importation of such Persons as any of the States now existing shall think proper to admit, shall not be prohibited by the Congress prior to the Year one thousand eight hundred and eight, but a Tax or duty may be imposed on such Importation, not exceeding ten dollars for each Person.

2 The Privilege of the Writ of Habeas Corpus shall not be suspended, unless when in Cases of Rebellion or Invasion the public Safety may require it.

3 No Bill of Attainder or ex post facto Law shall be passed.

4 No Capitation, or other direct, Tax shall be laid, unless in Proportion to the Census or Enumeration herein before directed to be taken.[5]

5 No Tax or Duty shall be laid on Articles exported from any State.

6 No Preference shall be given by any Regulation of Commerce or Revenue to the Ports of one State over those of another: nor shall Vessels bound to, or from, one State, be obliged to enter, clear, or pay Duties in another.

7 No Money shall be drawn from the Treasury, but in Consequence of Appropriations made by Law; and a regular Statement and Account of the Receipts and Expenditures of all public Money shall be published from time to time.

8 No Title of Nobility shall be granted by the United States; And no Person holding any Office of Profit or Trust under them, shall, without the Consent of the Congress, accept of any present, Emolument, Office, or Title, of any kind whatever, from any King, Prince, or foreign State.

Section 10   *1* No State shall enter into any Treaty, Alliance, or Confederation; grant Letters of Marque and Reprisal; coin Money; emit Bills of Credit; make any Thing but gold and silver Coin a Tender in Payment of Debts; pass any Bill of Attainder, ex post facto Law, or Law impairing the Obligation of Contracts, or grant any Title of Nobility.

2 No State shall, without the Consent of the Congress, lay any Imposts or Duties on Imports or Exports, except what may be absolutely necessary for executing its inspection Laws; and the net Produce of all Duties and Imposts, laid by any State on Imports or Exports, shall be for the Use of the Treasury of the United States; and all such Laws shall be subject to the Revision and Controul of the Congress.

3 No State shall, without the Consent of Congress, lay any Duty of Tonnage, keep Troops, or Ships of War in time of Peace, enter into any Agreement or Compact with another State, or with a foreign Power, or

[5] Modified by the Sixteenth Amendment.

engage in War, unless actually invaded, or in such imminent Danger as will not admit of delay.

ARTICLE II

Section 1 *1* The executive Power shall be vested in a President of the United States of America. He shall hold his office during the Term of four Years, and, together with the Vice President, chosen for the same Term, be elected, as follows.

2 Each State shall appoint, in such Manner as the Legislature thereof may direct, a Number of Electors, equal to the whole Number of Senators and Representatives to which the State may be entitled in the Congress: but no Senator or Representative, or Person holding an Office of Trust or Profit under the United States, shall be appointed an Elector.

3 The Electors shall meet in their respective States, and vote by Ballot for two Persons, of whom one at least shall not be an Inhabitant of the same State with themselves. And they shall make a List of all the Persons voted for, and of the Number of Votes for each; which List they shall sign and certify, and transmit sealed to the Seat of Government of the United States, directed to the President of the Senate. The President of the Senate shall, in the Presence of the Senate and House of Representatives, open all the Certificates, and the Votes shall then be counted. The Person having the greatest Number of Votes shall be the President, if such Number be a Majority of the whole Number of Electors appointed; and if there be more than one who have such Majority, and have an equal Number of Votes, then the House of Representatives shall immediately chuse by Ballot one of them for President; and if no Person have a Majority, then from the five highest on the List the said House shall in like Manner chuse the President. But in chusing the President, the Votes shall be taken by States, the Representation from each State having one Vote; A quorum for this Purpose shall consist of a Member or Members from two thirds of the States, and a Majority of all the States shall be necessary to a Choice. In every Case, after the Choice of the President, the Person having the greatest Number of Votes of the Electors shall be the Vice President. But if there should remain two or more who have equal Votes, the Senate shall chuse from them by Ballot the Vice President.[6]

4 The Congress may determine the Time of chusing the Electors, and the Day on which they shall give their Votes; which Day shall be the same throughout the United States.

5 No Person except a natural born Citizen, or a Citizen of the United States, at the time of the Adoption of this Constitution, shall be eligible to the Office of President; neither shall any Person be eligible to that Office who shall not have attained to the Age of thirty five Years, and been fourteen Years a Resident within the United States.

6 In Case of the Removal of the President from Office, or of his Death, Resignation, or Inability to discharge the Powers and Duties of the said Office, the Same shall devolve on the Vice President, and the Congress

[6]This paragraph was replaced in 1804 by the Twelfth Amendment.

may by Law provide for the Case of Removal, Death, Resignation, or Inability, both of the President and Vice President, declaring what officer shall then act as President, and such Officer shall act accordingly, until the Disability be removed, or a President shall be elected.

7 The President shall, at stated Times, receive for his Services, a Compensation, which shall neither be encreased nor diminished during the Period for which he shall have been elected, and he shall not receive within that Period any other Emolument from the United States, or any of them.

8 Before he enter on the Execution of his Office, he shall take the following Oath or Affirmation:—"I do solemnly swear (or affirm) that I will faithfully execute the Office of President of the United States, and will to the best of my Ability, preserve, protect and defend the Constitution of the United States."

Section 2   *1* The President shall be Commander in Chief of the Army and Navy of the United States, and of the Militia of the several States, when called into the actual Service of the United States; he may require the Opinion, in writing, of the principal Officer in each of the executive Departments, upon any Subject relating to the Duties of their respective Offices, and he shall have Power to grant Reprieves and Pardons for Offences against the United States, except in Cases of Impeachment.

2 He shall have Power, by and with the Advice and Consent of the Senate, to make Treaties, provided two thirds of the Senators present concur; and he shall nominate, and by and with the Advice and Consent of the Senate, shall appoint Ambassadors, other public Ministers and Consuls, Judges of the supreme Court, and all other Officers of the United States, whose Appointments are not herein otherwise provided for, and which shall be established by Law: but the Congress may by Law vest the Appointment of such inferior Officers, as they think proper, in the President alone, in the Courts of Law, or in the Heads of Departments.

3 The President shall have Power to fill up all Vacancies that may happen during the Recess of the Senate, by granting Commissions which shall expire at the End of their next Session.

Section 3   He shall from time to time give to the Congress Information of the State of the Union, and recommend to their Consideration such Measures as he shall judge necessary and expedient; he may, on extraordinary Occasions, convene both Houses, or either of them, and in Case of Disagreement between them, with Respect to the Time of Adjournment, he may adjourn them to such Time as he shall think proper; he shall receive Ambassadors and other public Ministers; he shall take Care that the Laws be faithfully executed, and shall Commission all the Officers of the United States.

Section 4   The President, Vice President and all civil Officers of the United States, shall be removed from Office on Impeachment for, and Conviction of, Treason, Bribery, or other high Crimes and Misdemeanors.

ARTICLE III

Section 1   The Judicial Power of the United States, shall be vested in one supreme Court, and in such inferior Courts as the Congress may from time to time ordain and establish. The Judges, both of the supreme and inferior Courts, shall hold their Offices during good Behaviour, and shall, at stated Times, receive for their Services, a Compensation, which shall not be diminished during their Continuance in Office.

Section 2   *1* The Judicial Power shall extend to all Cases, in Law and Equity, arising under this Constitution, the Laws of the United States, and Treaties made, or which shall be made, under their Authority;—to all Cases affecting Ambassadors, other public Ministers and Consuls;—to all Cases of admiralty and maritime Jurisdiction;—to Controversies to which the United States shall be a Party;—to Controversies between two or more States;—between a State and Citizens of another State;[7]—between Citizens of different States;—between Citizens of the same State claiming Lands under Grants of different States, and between a State, or the Citizens thereof, and foreign States, Citizens or Subjects.
2 In all Cases affecting Ambassadors, other public Ministers and Consuls, and those in which a State shall be Party, the supreme Court shall have original Jurisdiction. In all the other Cases before mentioned, the Supreme Court shall have appellate Jurisdiction, both as to Law and Fact, with such Exceptions, and under such Regulations as the Congress shall make.
3 The Trial of all Crimes, except in Cases of Impeachment, shall be by Jury; and such Trial shall be held in the State where the said Crimes shall have been committed; but when not committed within any State, the Trial shall be at such Place or Places as the Congress may by Law have directed.

Section 3   *1* Treason against the United States, shall consist only in levying War against them, or in adhering to their Enemies, giving them Aid and Comfort. No Person shall be convicted of Treason unless on the Testimony of two Witnesses to the same overt Act, or on Confession in open Court.
2 The Congress shall have Power to declare the Punishment of Treason, but no Attainder of Treason shall work Corruption of Blood, or Forfeiture except during the Life of the Person attainted.

ARTICLE IV

Section 1   Full Faith and Credit shall be given in each State to the public Acts, Records, and judicial Proceedings of every other State. And the Congress may by general Laws prescribe the Manner in which such Acts, Records and Proceedings shall be proved, and the Effect thereof.

[7] Restricted by the Eleventh Amendment.

Section 2   *1* The Citizens of each State shall be entitled to all Privileges and Immunities of Citizens in the several States.

2 A Person charged in any State with Treason, Felony, or other Crime, who shall flee from Justice, and be found in another State, shall on Demand of the executive Authority of the State from which he fled, be delivered up, to be removed to the State having Jurisdiction of the Crime.

3 No Person held to Service or Labour in one State, under the Laws thereof, escaping into another, shall, in Consequence of any Law or Regulation therein, be discharged from such Service or Labour, but shall be delivered up on Claim of the Party to whom such Service or Labour may be due.

Section 3   *1* New States may be admitted by the Congress into this Union; but no new State shall be formed or erected within the Jurisdiction of any other States; nor any State be formed by the Junction of two or more States, or Parts of States, without the Consent of the Legislatures of the States concerned as well as of the Congress.

2 The Congress shall have Power to dispose of and make all needful Rules and Regulations respecting the Territory or other Property belonging to the United States; and nothing in this Constitution shall be so construed as to Prejudice any Claims of the United States, or of any particular State.

Section 4   The United States shall guarantee to every State in this Union a Republican Form of Government, and shall protect each of them against Invasion; and on Application of the Legislature, or of the Executive (when the Legislature cannot be convened) against domestic Violence.

ARTICLE V

The Congress, whenever two thirds of both Houses shall deem it necessary, shall propose Amendments to this Constitution, or, on the Application of the Legislatures of two thirds of the several States, shall call a Convention for proposing Amendments, which, in either Case, shall be valid to all Intents and Purposes, as Part of this Constitution, when ratified by the Legislatures of three fourths of the several States, or by Conventions in three fourths thereof, as the one or the other Mode of Ratification may be proposed by the Congress; Provided that no Amendment which may be made prior to the Year One thousand eight hundred and eight shall in any Manner affect the first and fourth Clauses in the Ninth Section of the first Article; and that no State, without its Consent, shall be deprived of its equal Suffrage in the Senate.

ARTICLE VI

1 All Debts contracted and Engagements entered into, before the Adoption of this Constitution, shall be as valid against the United States under this Constitution, as under the Confederation.

2 This Constitution, and the Laws of the United States which shall be made in Pursuance thereof; and all Treaties made, or which shall be made, under the Authority of the United States, shall be the supreme Law of the Land; and the Judges in every State shall be bound thereby, any Thing in the Constitution or Laws of any State to the Contrary notwithstanding.

3 The Senators and Representatives before mentioned, and the Members of the several State Legislatures, and all executive and judicial Officers, both of the United States and of the several States, shall be bound by Oath or affirmation, to support this Constitution; but no religious Test shall ever be required as a Qualification to any Office or Public Trust under the United States.

ARTICLE VII

The Ratification of the Conventions of nine States, shall be sufficient for the Establishment of this Constitution between the States so ratifying the Same.

AMENDMENTS

AMENDMENT I

Congress shall make no law respecting an establishment of religion, or prohibiting the free exercise thereof; or abridging the freedom of speech, or of the press; or the right of the people peaceably to assemble, and to petition the Government for a redress of grievances.

AMENDMENT II

A well regulated Militia, being necessary to the security of a free State, the right of the people to keep and bear Arms, shall not be infringed.

AMENDMENT III

No Soldier shall, in time of peace be quartered in any house, without the consent of the Owner, nor in time of war, but in a manner to be prescribed by law.

AMENDMENT IV

The right of the people to be secure in their persons, houses, papers, and effects, against unreasonable searches and seizures, shall not be violated, and no Warrants shall issue, but upon probable cause, supported by Oath or affirmation, and particularly describing the place to be searched, and the persons or things to be seized.

AMENDMENT V

No person shall be held to answer for a capital, or otherwise infamous crime, unless on a presentment or indictment of a Grand Jury, except in cases arising in the land or naval forces, or in the Militia, when in actual service in time of War or public danger; nor shall any person be subject for the same offence to be twice put in jeopardy of life or limb; nor shall be compelled in any criminal case to be a witness against himself; nor be deprived of life, liberty, or property, without due process of law; nor shall private property be taken for public use, without just compensation.

AMENDMENT VI

In all criminal prosecutions the accused shall enjoy the right to a speedy and public trial, by an impartial jury of the State and district wherein the crime shall have been committed, which district shall have been previously ascertained by law, and to be informed of the nature and cause of the accusation; to be confronted with the witnesses against him; to have compulsory process for obtaining witnesses in his favor, and to have the Assistance of Counsel for his defence.

AMENDMENT VII

In suits at common law, where the value in controversy shall exceed twenty dollars, the right of trial by jury shall be preserved, and no fact tried by a jury shall be otherwise re-examined in any Court of the United States, than according to the rules of the common law.

AMENDMENT VIII

Excessive bail shall not be required, nor excessive fines imposed, nor cruel and unusual punishments inflicted.

AMENDMENT IX

The enumeration in the Constitution, of certain rights, shall not be construed to deny or disparage others retained by the people.

AMENDMENT X

The powers not delegated to the United States by the Constitution, nor prohibited by it to the States, are reserved to the States respectively, or to the people.

[The first ten Amendments were adopted in 1791.]

AMENDMENT XI

The Judicial power of the United States shall not be construed to extend to any suit in law or equity, commenced or prosecuted against one of the

United States by Citizens of another State, or by Citizens or Subjects of any Foreign State. [Adopted in 1798.]

AMENDMENT XII

The Electors shall meet in their respective states, and vote by ballot for President and Vice-President, one of whom, at least, shall not be an inhabitant of the same state with themselves; they shall name in their ballots the person voted for as President, and in distinct ballots the person voted for as Vice-President, and they shall make distinct lists of all persons voted for as President, and of all persons voted for as Vice-President, and of the number of votes for each, which lists they shall sign and certify, and transmit sealed to the seat of the government of the United States, directed to the President of the Senate;—The President of the Senate shall, in the presence of the Senate and House of Representatives, open all the certificates and the votes shall then be counted;—The person having the greatest number of votes for President, shall be the President, if such number be a majority of the whole number of Electors appointed; and if no person have such majority, then from the persons having the highest numbers not exceeding three on the list of those voted for as President, the House of Representatives shall choose immediately, by ballot, the President. But in choosing the President, the votes shall be taken by states, the representation from each state having one vote; a quorum for this purpose shall consist of a member or members from two-thirds of the states, and a majority of all the states shall be necessary to a choice. And if the House of Representatives shall not choose a President whenever the right of choice shall devolve upon them, before the fourth day of March next following, then the Vice-President shall act as President, as in the case of the death or other constitutional disability of the President.—The person having the greatest number of votes as Vice-President, shall be the Vice-President, if such number be a majority of the whole number of Electors appointed, and if no person have a majority, then from the two highest numbers on the list, the Senate shall choose the Vice-President; a quorum for the purpose shall consist of two-thirds of the whole number of Senators, and a majority of the whole number shall be necessary to a choice. But no person constitutionally ineligible to the office of President shall be eligible to that of Vice-President of the United States. [Adopted in 1804.]

AMENDMENT XIII

Section 1   Neither slavery nor involuntary servitude, except as a punishment for crime whereof the party shall have been duly convicted, shall exist within the United States, or any place subject to their jurisdiction.

Section 2   Congress shall have power to enforce this article by appropriate legislation. [Adopted in 1865.]

AMENDMENT XIV *citizenship of blacks*

Section 1   All persons born or naturalized in the United States, and subject to the jurisdiction thereof, are citizens of the United States and of the State wherein they reside. No State shall make or enforce any law which shall abridge the privileges or immunities of citizens of the United States; nor shall any State deprive any person of life, liberty, or property, without due process of law; nor deny to any person within its jurisdiction the equal protection of the laws.

Section 2   Representatives shall be apportioned among the several States according to their respective numbers, counting the whole number of persons in each State, excluding Indians not taxed. But when the right to vote at any election for the choice of electors for President and Vice President of the United States, Representatives in Congress, the Executive and Judicial officers of a State, or the members of the Legislature thereof, is denied to any of the male inhabitants of such State, being twenty-one years of age, and citizens of the United States, or in any way abridged, except for participation in rebellion, or other crime, the basis of representation therein shall be reduced in the proportion which the number of such male citizens shall bear to the whole number of male citizens twenty-one years of age in such State.

Section 3   No person shall be a Senator or Representative in Congress, or elector of President and Vice President, or hold any office, civil or military, under the United States, or under any State, who, having previously taken an oath, as a member of Congress, or as an officer of the United States, or as a member of any State legislature, or as an executive or judicial officer of any State, to support the Constitution of the United States, shall have engaged in insurrection or rebellion against the same, or given aid or comfort to the enemies thereof. But Congress may by a vote of two-thirds of each House, remove such disability.

Section 4   The validity of the public debt of the United States, authorized by law, including debts incurred for payment of pensions and bounties for services in suppressing insurrection or rebellion, shall not be questioned. But neither the United States nor any State shall assume or pay any debt or obligation incurred in aid of insurrection or rebellion against the United States, or any claim for the loss or emancipation of any slave; but all such debts, obligations and claims shall be held illegal and void.

Section 5   The Congress shall have power to enforce, by appropriate legislation, the provisions of this article. [Adopted in 1868.]

AMENDMENT XV

Section 1   The right of citizens of the United States to vote shall not be denied or abridged by the United States or by any State on account of race, color, or previous condition of servitude. *right to vote blacks*

Section 2   The Congress shall have power to enforce this article by appropriate legislation. [Adopted in 1870.]

AMENDMENT XVI   *Congress power to taxes*

The Congress shall have power to lay and collect taxes on incomes, from whatever source derived, without apportionment among the several States, and without regard to any census or enumeration. [Adopted in 1913.]

AMENDMENT XVII   *Senators tenure*

The Senate of the United States shall be composed of two Senators from each State, elected by the people thereof, for six years; and each Senator shall have one vote. The electors in each State shall have the qualifications requisite for electors of the most numerous branch of the State legislatures.

When vacancies happen in the representation of any State in the Senate, the executive authority of such State shall issue writs of election to fill such vacancies: *Provided,* That the legislature of any State may empower the executive thereof to make temporary appointments until the people fill the vacancies by election as the legislature may direct.

This amendment shall not be so construed as to affect the election or term of any Senator chosen before it becomes valid as part of the Constitution. [Adopted in 1913.]

AMENDMENT XVIII   *prohibition*

Section 1   After one year from the ratification of this article the manufacture, sale, or transportation of intoxicating liquors within, the importation thereof into, or the exportation thereof from the United States and all territory subject to the jurisdiction thereof for beverage purposes is hereby prohibited.

Section 2   The Congress and the several States shall have concurrent power to enforce this article by appropriate legislation.

Section 3   This article shall be inoperative unless it shall have been ratified as an amendment to the Constitution by the legislatures of the several States, as provided in the Constitution, within seven years from the date of the submission hereof to the States by the Congress. [Adopted in 1919.]

AMENDMENT XIX   *women suffrage*

The right of citizens of the United States to vote shall not be denied or abridged by the United States or by any State on account of sex.

Congress shall have power to enforce this article by appropriate legislation. [Adopted in 1920.]

AMENDMENT XX   *Congress*

Section 1   The terms of the President and Vice President shall end at noon at the 20th day of January, and the terms of Senators and Representatives at noon on the 3d day of January, of the years in which such terms would have ended if this article had not been ratified; and the terms of their successors shall then begin.

Section 2   The Congress shall assemble at least once in every year, and such meeting shall begin at noon on the 3d day of January, unless they shall by law appoint a different day.

Section 3   If, at the time fixed for the beginning of the term of the President, the President elect shall have died, the Vice President elect shall become President. If a President shall not have been chosen before the time fixed for the beginning of his term, or if the President elect shall have failed to qualify, then the Vice President elect shall act as President until a President shall have qualified; and the Congress may by law provide for the case wherein neither a President elect nor a Vice President elect shall have qualified, declaring who shall then act as President, or the manner in which one who is to act shall be selected, and such person shall act accordingly until a President or Vice President shall have qualified.

Section 4   The Congress may by law provide for the case of the death of any of the persons from whom the House of Representatives may choose a President whenever the right of choice shall have devolved upon them, and for the case of the death of any of the persons from whom the Senate may choose a Vice President whenever the right of choice shall have devolved upon them.

Section 5   Sections 1 and 2 shall take effect on the 15th day of October following the ratification of this article.

Section 6   This article shall be inoperative unless it shall have been ratified as an amendment to the Constitution by the legislatures of three-fourths of the several States within seven years from the date of its submission. [Adopted in 1933.]

AMENDMENT XXI   *repeals prohibition*

Section 1   The eighteenth article of amendment to the Constitution of the United States is hereby repealed.

Section 2   The transportation or importation into any State, Territory, or possession of the United States for delivery or use therein of intoxicating liquors, in violation of the laws thereof, is hereby prohibited.

Section 3   This article shall be inoperative unless it shall have been ratified as an amendment to the Constitution by conventions in the several States, as provided in the Constitution, within seven years from the date of the submission hereof to the States by the Congress. [Adopted in 1933.]

AMENDMENT XXII *tenure of office*

Section 1 No person shall be elected to the office of the President more than twice, and no person who has held the office of President, or acted as President, for more than two years of a term to which some other person was elected President shall be elected to the office of the President more than once. But this Article shall not apply to any persons holding the office of President when this Article was proposed by the Congress, and shall not prevent any person who may be holding the office of President, or acting as President, during the term within which this Article becomes operative from holding the office of President or acting as President during the remainder of such term.

Section 2 This Article shall be inoperative unless it shall have been ratified as an amendment to the Constitution by the legislatures of three-fourths of the several States within seven years from the date of its submission to the states by the Congress. [Adopted in 1951.]

AMENDMENT XXIII *elector apportionment*

Section 1 The District constituting the seat of Government of the United States shall appoint in such manner as the Congress may direct:
A number of electors of President and Vice President equal to the whole number of Senators and Representatives in Congress to which the District would be entitled if it were a State, but in no event more than the least populous states; they shall be in addition to those appointed by the States, but they shall be considered, for the purposes of the election of President and Vice President, to be electors appointed by a State; and they shall meet in the District and perform such duties as provided by the twelfth article of amendment.

Section 2 The Congress shall have power to enforce this article by appropriate legislation. [Adopted in 1961].

AMENDMENT XXIV *right to vote*

Section 1 The right of citizens of the United States to vote in any primary or other election for President or Vice President, for electors for President or Vice President, or for Senator or Representative in Congress, shall not be denied or abridged by the United States or any State by reason of failure to pay poll tax or other tax.

Section 2 The Congress shall have power to enforce this article by appropriate legislation. [Adopted in 1964.]

AMENDMENT XXV   *Succession in office*

Section 1   In case of the removal of the President from office or of his death or resignation, the Vice President shall become President.

Section 2   Whenever there is a vacancy in the office of the Vice President, the President shall nominate a Vice President who shall take office upon confirmation by a majority vote of both Houses of Congress.

Section 3   Whenever the President transmits to the President pro tempore of the Senate and the Speaker of the House of Representatives his written declaration that he is unable to discharge the powers and duties of his office, and until he transmits to them a written declaration to the contrary, such powers and duties shall be discharged by the Vice President as Acting President.

Section 4   Whenever the Vice President and a majority of either the principal officers of the executive departments or of such other body as Congress may by law provide, transmit to the President pro tempore of the Senate and the Speaker of the House of Representatives their written declaration that the President is unable to discharge the powers and duties of his office, the Vice President shall immediately assume the powers and duties of the office as Acting President.

Thereafter, when the President transmits to the President pro tempore of the Senate and the Speaker of the House of Representatives his written declaration that no inability exists, he shall resume the powers and duties of his office unless the Vice President and a majority of either the principal officers of the executive departments or of such other body as Congress may by law provide, transmit within four days to the President pro tempore of the Senate and the Speaker of the House of Representatives their written declaration that the President is unable to discharge the powers and duties of his office. Thereupon Congress shall decide the issue, assembling within forty-eight hours for that purpose if not in session. If the Congress, within twenty-one days after receipt of the latter written declaration, or if Congress is not in session, within twenty-one days after Congress is required to assemble, determines by two-thirds vote of both Houses that the President is unable to discharge the powers and duties of his office, the Vice President shall continue to discharge the same as Acting President; otherwise, the President shall resume the powers and duties of his office. [Adopted in 1967.]

AMENDMENT XXVI   *right to vote at 18*

Section 1   The rights of citizens of the United States, who are eighteen years of age or older, to vote shall not be denied or abridged by the United States or any state on account of age.

Section 2   The Congress shall have the power to enforce this article by appropriate legislation. [Adopted in 1971.]

AMENDMENT XXVII (Proposed) *ERA*

Section 1   Equality of rights under the law shall not be denied or abridged by the United States or by any state on account of sex.

Section 2   The Congress shall have the power to enforce, by appropriate legislation, the provisions of this article.

Section 3   This amendment shall take effect two years after the date of ratification. [Proposed by Congress on March 22, 1972.]

INDEX